The Mac OS X Leopard Book

How to do the things you want to do on your Mac

Scott Kelby

The Mac OS X Leopard Book

**The Mac OS X Leopard
Book Team**

CREATIVE DIRECTOR
Felix Nelson

TECHNICAL EDITORS
Kim Doty
Cindy Snyder
Terry White

TRAFFIC DIRECTOR
Kim Gabriel

PRODUCTION MANAGER
Dave Damstra

COVER DESIGN AND
CREATIVE CONCEPTS
Jessica Maldonado

STOCK PHOTOGRAPHY
COURTESY OF
iStockphoto.com

PUBLISHED BY
Peachpit Press

Copyright © 2008 by Scott Kelby

Composed in Myriad Pro (Adobe Systems Incorporated) and Lucida
Grande (Bigelow & Holmes Inc.) by Kelby Media Group.

Trademarks
All terms mentioned in this book that are known to be trademarks or
service marks have been appropriately capitalized. Peachpit Press cannot
attest to the accuracy of this information. Use of a term in the book should
not be regarded as affecting the validity of any trademark or service mark.

Macintosh, Mac, and Mac OS X Leopard are registered trademarks of
Apple Inc.

Warning and Disclaimer
This book is designed to provide information about Mac OS X Leopard.
Every effort has been made to make this book as complete and as accurate
as possible, but no warranty of fitness is implied.

The information is provided on an as-is basis. The author and Peachpit Press
shall have neither liability nor responsibility to any person or entity with
respect to any loss or damages arising from the information contained in
this book or from the use of the discs or programs that may accompany it.

ISBN 13: 978-0-321-54395-0
ISBN 10:   0-321-54395-5

9 8 7 6 5 4 3 2 1

Printed and bound in the United States of America

www.kelbytraining.com
www.peachpit.com

For the wonderful Kathy Siler,
who keeps an awful lot of plates
in the air so I have the time to
write books. You totally rock!

Acknowledgments

Although only one name appears on this book's spine, it takes a large, dedicated team of people to put a book like this together. Not only do I have the good fortune of working with such a great group of people, I now get the great pleasure of thanking them and acknowledging their hard work and dedication.

First, I'd like to thank my wonderful, amazing, hilarious, fun-filled, and loving wife, Kalebra. You're the best thing that's ever happened to me—you're part Wonder Woman, part supermom, part business exec, and part stand-up comic, and every day you manage to put a smile on my lips and a song in my heart. Your spirit, warmth, beauty, patience, and unconditional love continue to prove what everybody always says—I'm the luckiest guy in the world.

I also want to thank my 11-year-old son, Jordan. I'm so proud of him, so thrilled to be his dad, and I love watching him turn into the wonderful "little man" he has become. He has so many of his mother's special gifts, especially her boundless heart, and it's amazing the amount of joy he and his mom bring into my life.

Also, the single best thing that can happen to a person happened to me two years ago when God blessed our family with the birth of an adorable, happy, healthy, little baby girl—Kira. She's two now, and the single best thing that could've happened to her has already happened—she's a little clone of her mom. I couldn't ask for anything more.

Thanks to my big brother Jeff, for all the wonderful things you've done for me (and for other people) and for having so much of our dad in you. Your humor, generosity, and compassion are an inspiration. I love you, man.

Special thanks to one of my very best friends, and Mac guru on a scary level, Terry White. Anytime I come across a Mac question I can't answer, I call Terry, and darned if he doesn't know the answer. That's why I had to have Terry help tech edit this book. His ideas, input, and suggestions made this a far better book than it would have been, and once again, I am in his debt.

My heartfelt thanks go to my in-house editor and "wonder mom" Kim Doty, who makes writing these books so much fun for me. You've become such an important part of our team, and I'm really honored to get to work with you on these books.

Also, a big, big thanks to Cindy Snyder, who helps test all the techniques in the book, and as always, she caught lots of little things that others would have missed.

Thanks to my brilliant Creative Director Felix Nelson, for once again lending his creative ideas and input, which make every book we do that much better.

To my best buddy and book-publishing powerhouse Dave Moser (Hey you!), thank you for always insisting that we raise the bar and make everything we do better than anything we've done.

A big thanks to the amazingly creative and gifted Jessica Maldonado, for her great cover designs, her wonderfully creative art, and for never running out of the next cool idea. You rock!

Much love to my amazing layout team at Kelby Media Group, led by the mighty Dave Damstra, and a high five to Margie, Christy, Korman, Taffy, Leslie, and Nicole for just being so darn good at what you do.

I couldn't do any of this without the help and support of my wonderful assistant Kathy Siler, without whom I'd be sitting in my office mumbling and staring at the ceiling. She's my right-hand man (even though she's a woman) and makes my work life have order, calm, and sense. She is the best.

Thanks to my good friend Jean A. Kendra, for her support and enthusiasm for all my writing projects.

I owe a debt of gratitude to my friends at Peachpit Press, especially my publisher, Nancy Aldrich-Ruenzel, and my editor, Ted Waitt. They really "get it," and their philosophy and vision make writing books an awful lot of fun, which is very rare in this industry. Also my thanks to Scott Cowlin and Glenn Bisignani for tirelessly finding an audience for my books.

Thanks to my mentors, whose wisdom and whip-cracking have helped me immeasurably through-out my life, including John Graden, Jack Lee, Dave Gales, Judy Farmer, and Douglas Poole.

A personal thanks to my buddies Jeff Revell, Marvin Derezin, Rod Harlan, Mike Kubeisy, Dave Cross, Matt Kloskowski, Corey Barker, Rafael ("RC") Concepcion, John Couch, Vanelli, Tony Llanes, Scott Stahley, The Scriv, Terry White, Larry Becker, and Felix Nelson, just for being my buddies.

Thanks to the whole team at Kelby Media Group, for their commitment to excellence, for refusing to accept limitations, and for being an example of what's best about this industry.

And most importantly, an extra special thanks to God and His son Jesus Christ for always hearing my prayers, for always being there when I need Him, and for blessing me with such a wonderful life, and such a warm, loving family to share it with.

Other Books by Scott Kelby

The iPod Book

The iPhone Book

Mac OS X Killer Tips

Getting Started with Your Mac and Mac OS X Tiger

Macintosh: The Naked Truth

Scott Kelby's 7-Point System for Adobe Photoshop CS3

The Adobe Photoshop Lightroom Book for Digital Photographers

The Adobe Photoshop CS3 Book for Digital Photographers

The Photoshop Channels Book

Photoshop Down & Dirty Tricks

Photoshop Killer Tips

Photoshop Classic Effects

InDesign Killer Tips

The Digital Photography Book

The Digital Photography Book, vol. 2

The Photoshop Elements 6 Book for Digital Photographers

About the Author

Scott Kelby

Scott is Editor, Publisher, and co-founder of *Photoshop User* magazine, and Editor-in-Chief of *Layers* magazine. He is President and co-founder of the National Association of Photoshop Professionals (NAPP), the trade association for Adobe® Photoshop® users, and he's President of the software training, education, and publishing firm, Kelby Media Group.

Scott is a photographer, designer, and award-winning author of more than 40 books on technology and digital imaging, including *The iPod Book*, *The Digital Photography Book*, *The iPhone Book*, *Scott Kelby's 7-Point System for Adobe Photoshop CS3*, and *The Photoshop Book for Digital Photographers*. Scott has authored several best-selling Macintosh books, including *Mac OS X Killer Tips*, *Getting Started with Your Mac and OS X*, and the award-winning *Macintosh: The Naked Truth*, all from New Riders and Peachpit Press.

His books have been translated into dozens of different languages, including Chinese, Russian, Spanish, Korean, Polish, Taiwanese, French, German, Italian, Japanese, Dutch, Swedish, Turkish, and Portuguese, among others. For four years straight, Scott has been awarded the distinction of being the world's #1 best-selling author of all computer and technology books, across all categories.

Scott is Training Director for the Adobe Photoshop Seminar Tour, and Conference Technical Chair for the Photoshop World Conference & Expo. He is also featured in a series of training DVDs and online classes, and has been training creative professionals since 1993.

For more information on Scott, visit his daily blog, *Adobe® Photoshop® Insider,* at www.scottkelby.com.

Table of Contents

Chapter Three   63
Getting Your Life Organized
**Getting Your Contacts, Calendars,
and Other Stuff Set Up**

Table of Contents

Chapter Four   85
Unlocking Your Mac's Dashboard
How to Make Your Mac Bring You the Info You Need

Chapter Five   99
Getting Email on Your Mac
Plus, How to Leverage Your Mac's Mail to Keep Organized

Chapter Six   **125**
Music and Your Mac
You Can Do More Than Just Listen to Music;
You Can Make It, Too

Chapter Seven   **145**
Playing and Making Videos on Your Mac
Your Mac Is Half Movie Theater, Half Movie Studio.
Here's How to Use Both

Table of Contents

Chapter Eight   165
Managing Your Photos with iPhoto
How to Keep Track of, Organize, and Have Fun with Your Photos

Chapter Nine   195
Working with Photos on Your Mac
How to Make Your Still Images Come to Life

Table of Contents

Chapter Ten   211
Getting On the Internet
**Anyone Can *Look* at Webpages;
Now You Can Make Your Own!**

Chapter Zero
Seven Things You'll Wish You Had Known Before Reading This Book

(1) Here's how this book works: I wrote it as if you just got your Mac, came over to my house, and asked me to show you how to use it. When I'm with a friend, I skip the technical stuff and tell them how to do what they want to do. Like if you asked me, "Hey Scott, how can I delete a file from my Mac and make sure nobody else can easily retrieve it?" I wouldn't give you a lecture about file-encryption algorithms, or 128-bit decryption protocols. I'd say, "Just drag the file into your Mac's Trash, then go under the Finder menu and choose Secure Empty Trash." I'd tell you short and right to the point, and that's what I tried to do here.

(2) This is not a book strictly for beginners. The first chapter pretty much is, but the rest is for everybody—even people who have been using a Mac for a while. It's for people who just want to know how to do the things on their Mac they want to do. Each page covers only one topic, that way you can turn directly to the thing you want to do, and I tell you how to do just that one thing.

(3) How I teach you to use iMovie in just five pages: I decided early on that there was no way I could teach you everything about Apple's amazing iLife applications, like iMovie, iPhoto, Garage-Band, etc., and not make this an expensive 700-page book. So, I decided to just get you started. Give you just enough, so you could make your first iMovie, your first slide show, or create your first GarageBand song. Enough to let you experience what you can do with these brilliant applications. If you fall in love with one, then you can go buy one of those big thick books on it.

(4) I don't cover every topic. There were over 300 new features introduced in Leopard alone. Now, I didn't say there are 300 features in Leopard—there are 300 *new* features. So, I only covered the most popular topics—the ones you're most likely to use, and the ones I get asked about again and again.

(5) The intro page at the beginning of each chapter is designed to give you a quick mental break, and writing these off-the-wall chapter intros is kind of a tradition of mine (I do this in all my books). So if you're one of those really "serious" types, you can skip them because they'll just get on your nerves.

(6) This is a "show-me-how-to-do-it book." I'm telling you these tips like I'd tell a buddy. That means, oftentimes, it's just which button to click, which setting to change, which shortcut to use, and not a lot of reasons why. I figure that once you start getting comfortable with your Mac, you'll buy one of those "tell-me-all-about-it" Macintosh books. Now, it's almost time to get to work and I truly hope this book makes your Mac life easier and more fun. Beyond that, I hope it ignites your passion for using some of the amazingly creative tools Apple includes with every Mac (like iMovie, iPhoto, Photo Booth, and GarageBand, among others), and that you not only start doing the stuff you've always wanted to do, but that you uncover exciting new things you never dreamed of doing before.

(7) Special training videos just for you. I really want this stuff to stick, so I created a "recap" video for each chapter, where I quickly go over some of the chapter highlights (read the chapter first, then watch the video). You can find them at www.kelbytraining.com/books/leopardbook (here's the password: widget).

Chapter One

20 Things Every New Mac User Needs to Know

If You're New to the Mac, Start Here

 Okay, you probably noticed that the headline above says, "Every *New* Mac User," right? I know that some of you are probably thinking, "This isn't for me, I'm not a new user," and that's perfectly fine. "Old users" are welcome to read this chapter, too (however, if I had known you'd be coming, I would have used larger print, and made several references to World War II). Anyway, here's the thing: yes, this is a chapter aimed at new users, but don't think that there's nothing here for you old users. In fact, I have a perfect example: backing up. It's one of those things that everybody knows they should do regularly, but for some reason we just don't do it (it's kind of like flossing, but while you might not floss regularly, we know that Julia Roberts certainly does—we saw her flossing plenty in *Pretty Woman*). So even though we don't all back up, we have the best intention of doing so. Every rare once in a while I would run into somebody who actually backed up regularly, but now, thanks to Leopard, most of the people I know using Macs are actually backing up daily. Why? Because now it's finally easy. In fact, it's not just easy, it can be 100% automatic, with no input from you whatsoever. So, how do you set this automatic backup up? Gotcha! See, you do need this chapter, you old Mac user you! That's because some of the 20 things every new Mac user needs to know are also some things every old Mac user needs to know, too. So don't feel bad if you wind up secretly reading this chapter when nobody else is around. Your secret's safe with me. After all, look how many years I lived knowing that what's actually stored at Area 51 is Elvis' alien baby, yet I've never told a soul.

1. Working with Applications

Your Mac keeps your software programs in a folder called Applications, but it also puts quick links to the software programs it figures you're going to use the most down in the Dock at the bottom of your screen. If you move your cursor over any of the icons in the Dock, the name of the application pops up right above it. If you see an application you want to launch, just click on it and it launches (you know it's launching because its icon starts hopping up and down in the Dock for a few seconds). If the application you want to use doesn't appear in the Dock, go up to the top of the screen, click once on the Go menu, and then click on Applications to open the folder where all your Applications are stored. You can launch any of these applications by simply double-clicking on them. Now, if there's an application in that folder you think you'll be using a lot, just click-and-hold the mouse button on it, drag it right down to the Dock, and let go of the mouse button to add it to the Dock (now that application is always just one click away). If you want to quit an application, press-and-hold the Command key (it appears on both sides of your Spacebar), and then press the letter Q (for Quit). Every Mac application quits this way, so you might as well learn this keyboard shortcut now, because you'll be using it a lot.

2. Switching Between Applications

You can run more than one application at a time on your Mac (in fact, you can run as many as your computer has memory for), and you can tell which applications are currently running by looking down in the Dock. If you see a light blue dot under an application's icon, that means it's running. You can switch between running applications by either just going down to the Dock and clicking on any application that has that little blue dot below it, or you can press-and-hold the Command key (the keys on either side of your Space-bar), and then press the Tab key to bring up the Application Switcher. This is a list of all your running applications that appears in the center of your screen (well, it's not really a list, it's more of a row of icons, as seen above). Keep pressing-and-holding the Command key, and each time you press the Tab key, it switches to the next icon over. When you come to the icon for the application you want to switch to, just let go of those keys.

3. Using .Mac

Apple offers a very cool Web-based feature called .Mac (pronounced "dot Mac") that really extends the power of your Mac (the basic membership is $99.95 per year, but you can sign up for a free 60-day trial at www.mac.com). I tell anyone without their own website to get a .Mac account, because there is no easier way to put up a website, an online gallery, podcast, etc., than using your Mac's software, with the free integrated online Web hosting you get from .Mac. Anyone can have a great looking site up and running today, but that's just one feature of .Mac—I could go on and on, but if you go to mac.com, there are video demos that explain it all better than I can, so stop by there and you'll see what all the fuss is about. Now, if you've signed up for .Mac already, you can access your personal iDisk (your 10-gigabyte online storage disk) by going under the Go menu, under iDisk, and choosing My iDisk (or just use the keyboard shortcut Command-Shift-I). This puts your iDisk right on your desktop (just like your own hard disk—as shown above), and to look inside it, and put things on it, just double-click on it to open it and then drag-and-drop things right inside. Once you've put stuff there, you can have friends and family members access your iDisk from their Macs, or directly from the Web if they're PC users. For example, if you want to send a file to a friend (maybe it's a file or photo that's too large to email), first click-and-drag that file into your iDisk's Public folder (this is the one folder anyone can access), then let 'em know it's there, and they can go under the same Go menu and choose your iDisk, and it mounts on their computer. Incredibly handy.

4. Where to Save Your Files

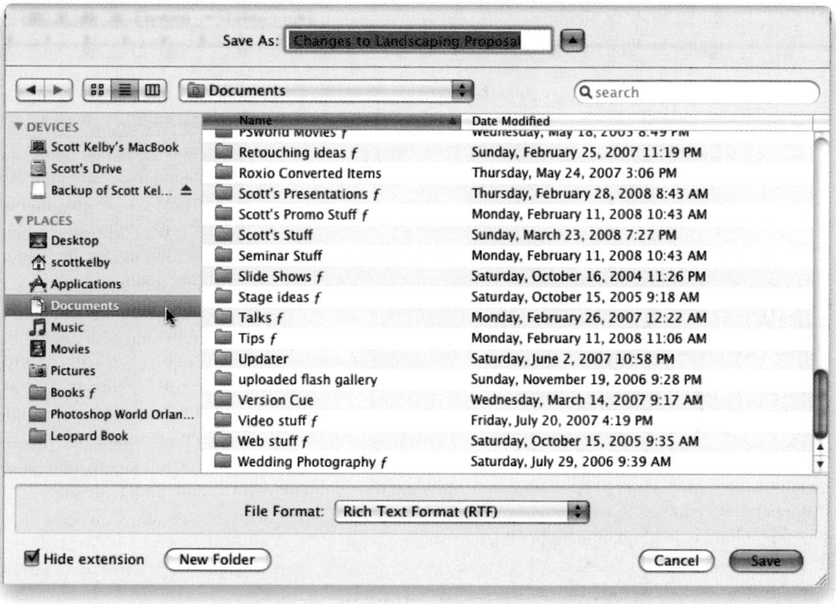

Save As: **Changes to Landscaping Proposal** ▲

📁 Documents ▼   🔍 search

Name	Date Modified
PSWorld Movies *f*	Wednesday, May 18, 2005 8:49 PM
📁 Retouching ideas *f*	Sunday, February 25, 2007 11:19 PM
📁 Roxio Converted Items	Thursday, May 24, 2007 3:06 PM
📁 Scott's Presentations *f*	Thursday, February 28, 2008 8:43 AM
📁 Scott's Promo Stuff *f*	Monday, February 11, 2008 10:43 AM
📁 Scott's Stuff	Sunday, March 23, 2008 7:27 PM
📁 Seminar Stuff	Monday, February 11, 2008 10:43 AM
📁 Slide Shows *f*	Saturday, October 16, 2004 11:26 PM
📁 Stage ideas *f*	Saturday, October 15, 2005 9:18 AM
📁 Talks *f*	Monday, February 26, 2007 12:22 AM
📁 Tips *f*	Monday, February 11, 2008 11:06 AM
📁 Updater	Saturday, June 2, 2007 10:58 PM
📁 uploaded flash gallery	Sunday, November 19, 2006 9:28 PM
📁 Version Cue	Wednesday, March 14, 2007 9:17 AM
📁 Video stuff *f*	Friday, July 20, 2007 4:19 PM
📁 Web stuff *f*	Saturday, October 15, 2005 9:35 AM
📁 Wedding Photography *f*	Saturday, July 29, 2006 9:39 AM

▼ DEVICES
📱 Scott Kelby's MacBook
💾 Scott's Drive
💿 Backup of Scott Kel... ⏏

▼ PLACES
🖥 Desktop
🏠 scottkelby
🅰 Applications
📄 Documents
🎵 Music
🎬 Movies
📷 Pictures
📁 Books *f*
📁 Photoshop World Orlan...
📁 Leopard Book

File Format: **Rich Text Format (RTF)** ▼

☑ Hide extension   (New Folder)   (Cancel)   (**Save**)

When you're done working in an application and you want to save your work, you can go under the File menu and choose Save, but since you'll be doing this (saving) a lot, you'll want to learn the keyboard shortcut now, which is Command-S. When you press Command-S, if it's the first time you've saved this file (in other words, you started from scratch with a blank page or blank document), then the Save As dialog will appear (think of "Save As" as short for "Save this file As [fill in with what you want to name the file]." There are no special naming rules, just name it whatever you want). So, once you've figured out what you want to name your file, the next big question is where do you want to save the file? If you want to make your life easy (and trust me, you do), save your files in your Documents folder. That way, you always know right where to look for your files (make sense, right?). The quickest way to make sure your files are saved in that Documents folder, is to click on it in the sidebar on the left (under Places), as shown above. Now, when you save your files here, it just tosses them in this big folder, so you might want to create a subfolder (a folder inside your Documents folder) to help keep things organized. To do that, just click on the New Folder button in the bottom-left corner of the Save As dialog. Well, now that you know where to save your documents, and how to create a subfolder to keep things organized, you can just click the Save button and your file is saved (and you know right where to go to find that file again later).

5. Clearing Window Clutter Using Exposé

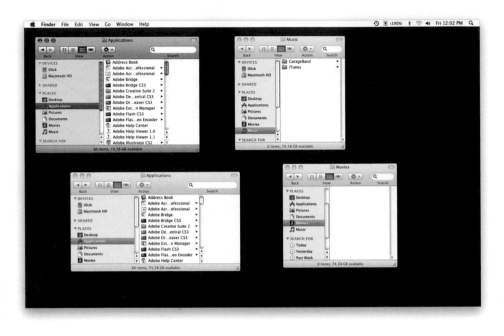

If you have a bunch of windows cluttering up your desktop and you can't find the one you want, try this: press the F10 key on your keyboard (Fn-F10 on a laptop or new, flat keyboard). This instantly arranges little versions of all the open windows in your current application onscreen at once (and dims everything else), so you can easily see each one clearly. Just click on the window you want, and it returns you to your regular desktop, with that window in front. This feature is called Exposé, and it works with active Finder windows or any active application. So if you have a bunch of windows open in Adobe InDesign or Safari, just press F10 and it does the same thing to those application windows. If you press F11 instead (Fn-F11 on a laptop or new keyboard), it temporarily hides all your open windows (so you have a clear view of the desktop), and when you press F11 again, they come back (if you press-and-hold the F11 key instead, they just stay hidden as long as you hold the key down). I use this press-and-hold-the-F11-key trick when I want to add an attachment to an email message. I press F11 to hide everything, then I go to my hard drive, find the file, click-and-hold on it, then I release the F11 button and I'm back in Mail, where I can drag-and-drop that file right into my message. Sweet! Now, here's a twist: if you press the F3 key (F9 on older keyboards), it does that "arranges little versions of all the open windows" thing, but to all your open windows, both in the Finder and your open applications, all at the same time, so you get the full view of everything happening on your Mac at once. You can assign different keys to Exposé by going to the System Preferences (found under the Apple menu). Click on Exposé & Spaces and then click on the Exposé tab.

6. Getting Back to Your Desktop

If you want to get back to your desktop, just press-and-hold the Option key and then click on the Finder icon in the Dock (it's the first icon). The reason I have you hold the Option key is this: if you're working in another application, and you just click the Finder icon, it opens a Finder window (over the application you're working on) with the contents of your Home folder. Sometimes you want access to that folder, but it seems like every time I tell a new user to click on the Finder icon, and that folder shows up, they say, "No, I just want to get back to where the hard drive icon is on my desktop background." That's why I now tell everybody to Option-click on the Finder icon—pressing-and-holding that Option key tells your Mac to hide everything else and show you your desktop (it still opens that Home folder, but at least you're back at your desktop now). There is another way to reach your desktop, and that is to click anywhere on it that's visible (so if you're working in an application, but you can see some of your desktop in the background, just click on it and it takes you to it. However, you'll only be able to work with things on the desktop you can see (in other words, your open applications will still be visible). So, to hide those applications (and see your whole desktop), after clicking on your desktop, press Command-Option-H. Now, you're probably thinking, "Wouldn't it be easier just to Option-click the Finder icon?" Yup. That's why I told you that one first, but now if you're tempted to just click on the desktop (because you can see it), you'll know how to hide the other junk once you're there.

7. Working with Finder Windows

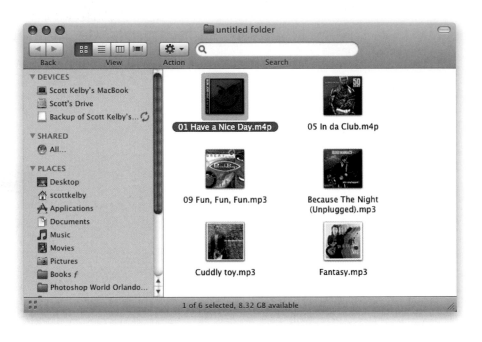

When you open a folder on your Mac, it opens up in a floating window. To move the window, just click on the bar across the top and drag it where you want it. To close a window, you could click on the little red round Close button in the top-left corner, but it's quicker to use the keyboard shortcut Command-W (it's easy to remember—W for window). To have a window automatically resize so it displays as much of its contents as possible, click the little green Expand button up in the top-left corner of the window and it will expand. When you open multiple windows, the last window you opened appears in front, and the rest are stacked behind it. To bring any window to the front, just click on it. To move windows that are behind the one in front, just press-and-hold the Command key first, then click-and-drag the top of those back windows and move 'em where you want 'em. If you want to keep a window handy (in other words, you don't want to close it, but you don't need it cluttering up your desktop right now), you can kind of park it in the Dock until you need it. Just click on the little yellow round Minimize button in the top-left corner (or use the keyboard shortcut Command-M), which puts it in the Dock—just one click away whenever you need to open it again.

8. Finding Files on Your Mac

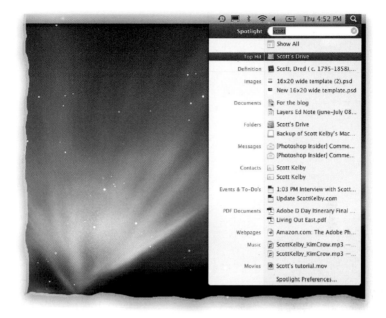

You find stuff on your Mac using Spotlight—just click once on the magnifying glass icon up in the top-right corner of your screen and a little search field pops down. Type in what you're looking for (you don't need the exact name of the file—any word in the filename will do). As soon as you start typing, it starts searching and shows you the top five results of its search (in each category) right below the search field. But it doesn't just search filenames, it searches everything (and I mean everything), including inside your emails, photos, and documents. It searches in your address book, calendar, songs—anywhere it can look to help you find what you're looking for fast. If you see the file you were searching for in the results list, just click on it and it opens. Now, if you don't see the file you were looking for in that list, click Show All up at the top of the list, and a window opens with all the results that match your search word. You can choose to show just the files whose name matches (click the File Name button up top), or have it search through the contents of every file (click the Contents button).

⋉ MacTip: Searching Inside Your Mac's Applications

Spotlight is built right into Mail, iCal, Address Book, and any Apple application where you'd need to search for stuff. Just type a word or name right in the search field within that application, and it does a Spotlight search of just that application, and shows the results of your search in that application's main window.

9. Adding Things to Your Sidebar

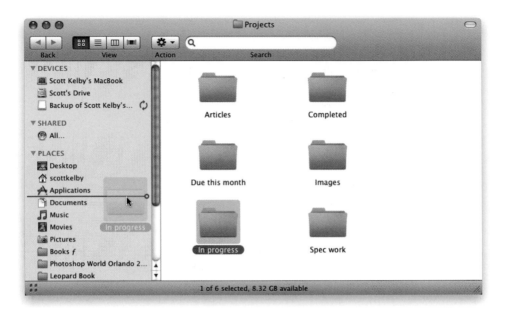

The sidebar is on the left side of every Finder window and is there to put the things you use the most one click away (so think of it like the Dock, but instead of being for applications, it's for files and folders you use a lot). For example, when I'm working on a project for a few weeks, I put that folder in the sidebar so I'm always just one click away from it. Also, if it's there in the sidebar, I can click-and-drag files right into the sidebar folder and they're added to the real folder, so it's incredibly handy having it right there. To add a file or folder to the sidebar, just click on it in the Finder window and drag it to the sidebar under Places. To remove it, just click-and-drag it right off the sidebar (doing this just removes the quick link to it from the sidebar—it doesn't delete the real folder or file).

X MacTip: Changing Your Mac's Volume

You can change your Mac's volume with the little speaker icon at the top-right side of your screen—click on it and a little volume slider pops down. If you're running a slide show or full-screen movie and can't get to that little slider, then use the Volume keys (the ones with speaker icons on them on your Mac's keyboard. If you use a MacBook, MacBook Pro, or MacBook Air, the F10 key mutes the volume, F11 lowers the volume, and F12 raises it). When you press these keys, you'll see the speaker icon appear on your screen.

10. Deleting Files from Your Mac

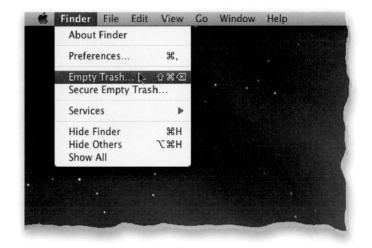

If you want to remove (delete) a file from your Mac, it's actually a two-step process: (1) drag-and-drop the file onto the Trash icon that lives at the end of your Dock. When you do that, you're basically saying, "I intend to throw everything in this trash can away soon, but not yet." That way, you can still pull something out of the trash, if you change your mind, by double-clicking on the Trash icon—it will open just like any other Finder window. Find the file you changed your mind about deleting, and click-and-drag it out of the trash. But the second step, (2) emptying the trash, really does delete your file (and any other files waiting in the trash along with it). To do that, you go under the Finder menu and choose Empty Trash. Now it's really gone.

X **MacTip: Deleting Files So They Can't Be Recovered**

If you need to delete a private or sensitive document and want to make sure it can't easily be retrieved by a Mac expert or IT person using file recovery software, then instead of choosing Empty Trash, choose Secure Empty Trash from the Finder menu.

11. Keeping Things Organized

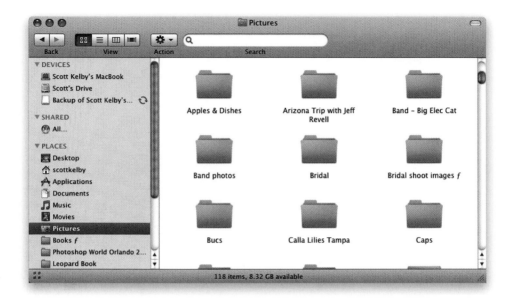

Your Mac will wind up with literally thousands of files on it in no time, and you'll want to be able to get to the stuff you need without having to run a Spotlight search every time you need a file, right? So, although this is going to sound simple, and kind of obvious, I can't tell you how many people don't follow this simple rule: save any music files you download or create in your Mac's Music folder; save your movies in your Movies folder; save your photos in your Pictures folder; and like I mentioned earlier in this chapter, save all your other files in your Documents folder. That way, you're always just one click away from getting near your stuff (it's only one click, because Apple puts these folders in the sidebar of every Finder window). Now, you can have as many subfolders as you'd like inside of these folders. For example, your Pictures folder can have folders inside of it like Family Photos, Travel Photos, Fine Art Photos, etc., but the key thing is, all your photos go inside that main Pictures folder. Once you've done this, when you open your Pictures folder, you'll notice that there's a Spotlight search field at the top of the window. To search through your entire Mac, just type a word in there and it starts searching, but you can instantly narrow that search down to just your Pictures folder by double-clicking on it at the top of that window once the search begins. Believe me, remembering to save the right files in the right folders like this will make your Mac life easier, and keep you more organized.

12. Renaming Stuff

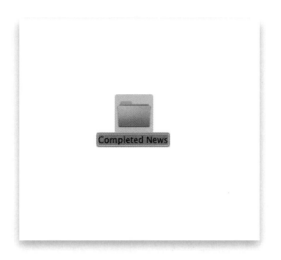

If you want to rename a file, a folder, or even your Mac's hard disk, just click on it to select it, then press the Return key on your keyboard. This highlights the name field, and you can just type in a new name. When you're done, hit the Return key again.

X MacTip: How to Make a Copy of a File

To make a copy of a file you see on your Mac, just click on it, then go under the File menu and choose Duplicate (or use the keyboard shortcut, Command-D). This makes a copy of the file, and automatically adds the word "copy" to the end of the filename, so you know it's a copy.

13. Setting Up a Wireless Bluetooth Device

Bluetooth

Show All

"Scott Kelby's MacBook" is the name Bluetooth devices use to connect to this computer

☑ On   ☑ Discoverable

Scott Kelby's iPhone
● Not Connected

Type **Smartphone**
Services **None**
Paired **No**
Connected ● **No**

☑ Show Bluetooth status in the menu bar

Advanced... ⑦

If you're using a wireless keyboard or wireless mouse, you don't have to worry—your Mac will find these automatically and handle all the connections for you, but if you want to connect a non-Apple Bluetooth device (like a wireless phone or PDA), then go under the Apple menu and choose System Preferences. Click on the Bluetooth icon (it's the first icon in the second row under Hardware) to bring up the dialog you see above, and then click the Set Up New Device button (in the center of the dialog) if you don't have anything wireless connected yet, or click the little + (plus sign) button (circled above in red) if you already have something wireless connected, which will bring up the Bluetooth Setup Assistant dialog. This will lead you through the steps for connecting your phone, PDA, etc.—just answer the questions it asks, and it'll take care of the rest.

⌧ MacTip: Putting Your Mac to Sleep

If you're going to be away from your Mac for just a bit, put it to sleep by going under the Apple menu and choosing Sleep, or by pressing the power button once. To wake your Mac from sleep, just press a key or move the mouse (on a laptop, just open the lid, if you closed it). This wakes your Mac right where you left off— all your applications and documents are still open, just like you left them.

14. Password Protecting Your Mac

If you use your Mac at work and you go out for lunch, your Mac is pretty much wide open for a co-worker to sit down and start nosing around in your stuff. That's why you might want to add password protection to your screen saver. That way, if you walk away from your Mac long enough to where your screen saver kicks in (or you put your Mac to sleep), everybody is locked out of it unless they know the password. To turn this feature on, go under the Apple menu and choose System Preferences. In the System Preferences dialog, click on Security (at the top, under Personal) and in the Security preferences dialog, click on the General tab. Turn on the checkbox for Require Password to Wake This Computer from Sleep or Screen Saver (as shown above), and close the dialog by pressing Command-W. Now, if someone tries to wake your Mac from sleep, or access it while the screen saver is on, it will ask for your login password. If they don't know it, they don't get in—simple as that.

X MacTip: Logging Out vs. Password Protecting Your Screen Saver

If you don't want to password protect your screen saver/Sleep function (as shown above), you could go under the Apple menu and choose Log Out (it's at the bottom of the menu), but the problem is, while it's easy to remember to do that at lunchtime, it doesn't protect you if you get stopped for a few minutes on your way back from the restroom, or pulled into an impromptu meeting, or any of a dozen things that happen during the day.

15. Backing Up Your Mac

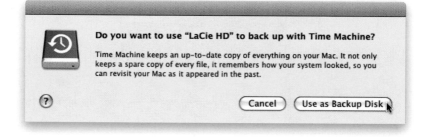

I tell every Mac-using friend I know, "You absolutely, positively must have a regular backup of all the stuff on your Mac," because hard drives (not just on Macs—on all computers of every kind) do go bad (crash). It's not a matter of *if* your hard drive will crash; it's a matter of *when* it will crash, because one day it just will. It's happened to just about every computer user on earth (and if you meet one who swears it never has—it's only because it hasn't happened *yet*). Your Mac has an absolutely brilliant built-in backup feature called Time Machine, and to have it back up your Mac, all you have to do is plug an external hard drive into your Mac, and it will ask you if you want to use this hard drive as your Time Machine backup. Click Use as Backup Disk, and it will back up everything on your Mac (the first time you back up is usually an overnight deal, so do this before you hit the sack. From then on, it just backs up things that have changed since your last backup, so it hardly takes any time at all). So, how often should you back up? Once a day (just plug in that external hard drive once a day, and Time Machine will do all the work—it won't even ask you, it will just back up for you. It's a totally automated deal and requires nothing from you other than remembering to plug in the hard drive. If you keep it plugged in all the time, you'll always be backed up). Now, if you're like me (and you forget to back up), then you might consider Apple's wireless hard drive, Time Capsule, which does automatic hourly Time Machine backups for you (you don't have to remember to plug anything in). It's completely invisible to you and you're always backed up (you can find more information about Time Capsule at www.apple.com). You'll love it.

16. Retrieving Lost Files Using Time Machine

If you deleted a file a few days, weeks, or even months ago, as long as you've been backing up using Time Machine, you can go back in time and retrieve that file. First, start by opening a Finder window, and then type in the word you want to search for up in the search field in the top-right corner of the window. Once the results show up, of course, make sure the file you want isn't really there. Then make sure your backup drive is connected to your Mac, and click on the Time Machine icon in your Dock (or Applications folder) to launch it. In a moment, Time Machine will take over your screen and start searching for you, but you have to tell it how far back to search, so use the two arrows (near the bottom-right corner of the screen) to search back day-by-day in time (or use the timeline on the right side of the screen). When you get to a day that has the file you need (probably the day before you threw it away, right?), click on it, then click the Restore button in the bottom-right corner, and it retrieves that file from the backup drive and puts it on your Mac. I know—amazing isn't it?

X MacTip: Two Button Shortcuts You Need to Know

When a dialog pops up on your Mac, the button you're most likely to push is highlighted in blue and is softly glowing. Rather than grabbing the mouse and clicking it, you can press the Return key and it will click the blue glowing button for you. If you don't want the blue button, and you want the Cancel button instead, just press the Esc key on your keyboard (it's called the Escape key).

17. What to Do If an Application Freezes

Every once in a while, for one reason or another, an application will freeze up—you go to do something and you get a spinning "beach ball" (as we call it). If that happens, press-and-hold the Option key, then go to that application's icon in the Dock and click-and-hold on it to bring up a pop-up menu. If it is indeed frozen, you'll see the phrase Application Not Responding in gray letters at the top of the menu. In that case, choose Force Quit from the bottom of that menu. That will usually force the application to quit, so you can restart it. The only downside to force quitting is if you had a document open in that application before it froze and hadn't saved it in a while, then you'll lose any unsaved changes in that document. By the way, you save changes to an open document by pressing Command-S (I do every few minutes, or right after I've done anything major that I don't want to lose). Now, in some rare instances, you'll choose Force Quit this way, and it doesn't quit the program. In that case, go under the Apple menu and choose Force Quit (or just press Command-Option-Esc). This brings up the dialog you see above, which lists all your running applications. Click on the one that won't quit and then click the Force Quit button to do the trick.

18. Fixing Problems with Your Mac

If you're having trouble with your Mac (something's not working right, or something just isn't working like you think it should be), I'll bet I can help you fix it—just restart your Mac. That's right, go under the Apple menu and choose Restart, and as weird as this may sound, about 90% of the everyday problems that might occur on your Mac can be fixed by simply restarting it (that's actually pretty cool when you think about it). If a restart doesn't do the trick, go under the Go menu and choose Utilities, and then inside the Utilities folder, click on Disk Utility to launch it. When the dialog appears, click on your hard disk in the list on the left, then click on the First Aid tab, and then click the Repair Disk Permissions button (shown circled above in red). Now, if doing both of those still hasn't fixed your problem, then next I'd go to www.apple.com/support/leopard (which is Apple's excellent online support area) and see if the answer is there. My last resort is to put my Mac in my car and drive to the nearest Apple Retail Store, where they offer excellent in-house repair.

X MacTip: What to Do If Your Mac Freezes Up and You Can't Restart

It's rare, but it's possible that your Mac will temporarily freeze up, and you won't be able to go under the Apple menu to restart it. If that's the case, just press-and-hold the power button on your Mac for three or four seconds, and it forces it to power down (a full instant shut down). Release the button, press it again once, and your Mac will restart.

19. Burning Files to CD or DVD

If you want to burn some files to a CD or DVD, you have two choices: (1) a down-and-dirty style burn, where you just click on a file (or Command-click to select multiple files), then go under the File menu and choose Burn to Disc, or if you want a level of organization to your disc, then (2) create a Burn folder first, so you can arrange the files in the order and view you'd like them to appear. To create a Burn folder, just go under the File menu and choose New Burn Folder. This adds a new folder to your desktop with a little radio-activity icon on it. Click-and-drag any files you want burned to disc onto this folder, and then double-click on the folder to open it and arrange the view, order, etc. (by the way, it doesn't actually move the files into this folder, instead it makes aliases, which are just pointers to the real files that remain where they are). Once they're in the order you'd like, click the Burn button in the upper-right corner of the window, and it will prompt you to insert a blank CD, as shown above (if your files total less than 700MB), or a DVD (if they're larger—up to 4GB). When you insert a disc, a window will appear asking you to name your disc, so type in a name, then click the Burn button and it does the rest. (*Note*: To burn a DVD, your Mac must have a SuperDrive or be connected to an external DVD-burning drive.)

20. How to Set Up a Printer

The first step is to connect your printer to your Mac (they usually connect with a specially-designed USB cable or FireWire cable, but sadly that cable usually doesn't come included with the printer, so check when you buy your printer). Most likely, your Mac will recognize your printer (Leopard has hundreds of the most popular print drivers already installed), and it will automatically do all the configuring for you. So, to print a document, you press Command-P (it's the same shortcut in every program) and the Print dialog appears. Now, by default, it doesn't show you all the options you see in the Print dialog above—to get to those options, click the little blue arrow button to the immediate right of the Printer pop-up menu, which is the same menu where you choose your printer. If, for some reason, your Mac doesn't recognize your printer (it doesn't appear in the Printer pop-up menu), then you'll need to install the printer driver for your printer. These usually come on a CD in the printer's shipping box, but rather than using the one on disc (which is sometimes outdated), I generally go and download the latest version of the printer driver from the printer manufacturer's website (they're free to download and install when you double-click on them). Once the printer driver is installed, open a document, press Command-P, and in the Print dialog, from the Printer pop-up menu, choose Add Printer. A dialog will appear where you can click on your printer (or choose it from the Print Using pop-up menu at the bottom), and then click the Add button. Now your printer will be added to the regular Printer pop-up menu, and you won't have to go through that Add Printer stuff again.

More Tips for Using Your Mac

X MacTip: Get to What You Want in Any Menu Faster

If you're in a menu, you can jump directly to what you want by pressing the first letter of the menu item. For example, if you're under the Finder's View menu, and you want to open View Options, press the letter V and hit the Return key. If two items start with the same letter (like under the Apple menu, where pressing S selects Shut Down, rather than System Preferences), then type the first two letters (to open System Preferences, type SY, and then press Return).

X MacTip: Keeping Info on More Than One Mac Synced Up

If you have more than one Mac, and you signed up for a .Mac account, then you can use it to keep your Macs synced (so both Macs always have the same bookmarks, addresses, calendar info, etc.). Just go to the System Preferences, and click on the .Mac icon (it's in the third row). Once you're signed in, click on the Sync tab and turn on the Synchronize with .Mac checkbox to upload this computer's info to .Mac. Turn on the checkboxes next to the items that you want to sync and then turn on the Show Status in Menu Bar checkbox at the bottom, which adds a little pop-up menu to your menu bar (a circle with two arrows), so you can sync right from the menu bar. Close System Preferences then do the same thing with your other Mac, and choose Sync Now from that little pop-up menu. That's it!

X MacTip: Moving Everything from One Mac to Another Mac

If you wind up buying a new Mac, or you want two Macs that are exactly the same in every way, you can use the Migration Assistant (it's found in your Utilities folder within your Applications folder) to do this for you, and it really works brilliantly. It takes all your email, passwords, accounts, bookmarks, applications—everything—and moves it from one Mac to another Mac all automatically. You just need a FireWire cable (available from Apple's online store, or almost any computer store) to connect the two Macs, then launch the Migration Assistant and follow a couple of simple onscreen instructions. It couldn't be easier.

X MacTip: Changing the Size of Your Sidebar

You can change how wide any Finder window's sidebar is by hovering your cursor over the line that separates the sidebar from the rest of the window. Your cursor will change into a bar with two arrows. Now you can click-and-drag the sidebar wider or thinner.

⚡More Tips for Using Your Mac

X MacTip: Finding the Location of a File Using Spotlight

If you do a Spotlight search and see a list pop down of possible matches, there are two things you'll want to know: (1) If you hover your cursor over one of the search results in the list, a window will pop up showing the location of that file on your computer. If you click on the file, it will open it, but if you'd like to open the folder where that file is located, instead, then (2) press-and-hold the Command key, click on the item, and it will appear in a Finder window.

X MacTip: Turning Off the Empty Trash Warning

Each time you empty the Trash, you get a warning dialog asking if you're sure you want to delete the items in the Trash. If you want to skip that warning for now, just press-and-hold the Option key before you choose Empty Trash. If you never want to see that warning again, go under the Finder menu and choose Preferences, then click on the Advanced Icon and turn off the checkbox for Show Warning Before Emptying the Trash.

X MacTip: Using Spotlight as Your Dictionary

When you type a word in the Spotlight search field, as soon as you're done typing, the definition of the word appears near the top of the results list that pops down, right beside the word "Definition." Hover your cursor over the short definition, and it gives you a longer one. Click on it, and it opens your Mac's built-in dictionary and gives you the full definition.

X MacTip: Using Spotlight as a Shortcut to Your Applications

Want to quickly open an application that's not in your Dock? Just go up to Spotlight and type in the first three or four letters of the application's name, then press the Return key to launch the application (you'll see the application near the top of the results list that pops down). If you have more than one application that starts with the same letters, then you'll see them listed next to Application near the top of the Spotlight results list—just click on the one you want to launch it.

Chapter Two

Customizing Your Mac Your Way

How to Personalize Your Mac So It's More, Well…You!

One of my favorite things about the Mac is how customizable it is. You can choose your own custom desktop background, choose the alarm sounds it makes, use your own photos as a screen saver, and really make your Mac—your Mac! Now, there's a term that's commonly used today to describe the act of customizing things to the extreme (like cars, or TVs, or even Macs), and it's called "pimping." (Actually, it's probably spelled "pimpin'" but it drives book editors insane if you intentionally leave a letter off an otherwise perfectly spelled word.) In fact, there's a hit show on MTV called *Pimp My Ride,* and it's all about them taking some junky old car and "pimpin' it" with every customization imaginable, including flat panel TVs, huge chrome wheels, custom airbrushed paint jobs, and even things like built-in fish tanks and guitar amps. I hate to admit it, but I really like the show, and my 11-year-old son and I used to watch it together all the time, until one day he looked at me and said, "Dad, what's a pimp?" I was speechless. I guess it's because we had watched like 16 episodes together and the topic never came up, so I figured it wouldn't and then—BAM!—"Dad, what's a pimp?" Well, I thought I had a pretty clever way out by saying, "Let's look it up in my Mac's built-in dictionary," thinking there's no way it would be there, so I could say, "Gee, son—it's not here, so I don't know." But much to my chagrin, it popped up with, "pimp. noun. A man who controls prostitutes and arranges clients for them, taking part of their earnings in return." I cringed, and then he said, "Dad, what's a prostitute?" and I just panicked and said, "Go ask your mother," and he said quizzically, "Is she a prostitute?" and we never watched *Pimp My Ride* again.

Renaming Your Hard Disk

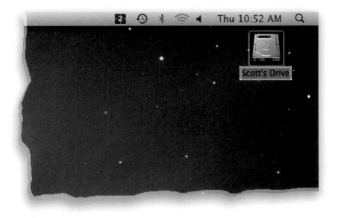

When your Mac comes from the factory, your hard disk is named "Macintosh HD" by default, but you can change it to any name you'd like by simply clicking on it (the Macintosh HD icon on your desktop), and then pressing the Return key. This highlights the name field so you can type in any name you'd like. When you're done, just press the Return key again.

Choosing a Different Desktop Background

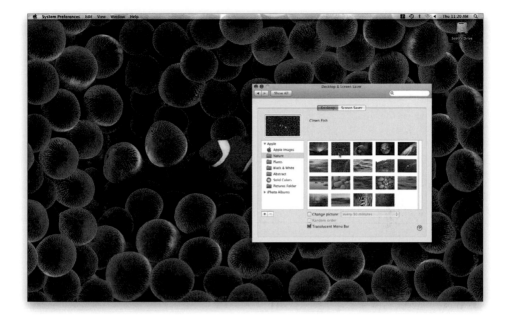

Mac OS X Leopard comes preset with a starfield desktop background (its official name is actually "Aurora"), but you can choose a different desktop background easily. Apple ships your Mac with a built-in collection of desktop backgrounds. To use one of these built-in desktop backgrounds, go under the Apple menu and choose System Preferences. When the System Preferences dialog appears, click on the Desktop & Screen Saver icon, and then when that pane appears, click on the Desktop tab at the top, and along the left side, under Apple, you'll see a list of folders (even the little Apple icon is a folder) of images you can choose from. Click on one of those folders and you'll see small thumbnails of the backgrounds in that folder appear in the right column. Click on any one to see an instant preview of how that image would look on your desktop. When you find an image you like, just close the System Preferences dialog by clicking on the round red Close button in the upper-left corner.

X MacTip: Change Desktop Images Automatically

If you get tired of having the same desktop background all day long, you can have Leopard choose a different background for you, anywhere from every 5 seconds (which makes a great prank to pull on a co-worker) up to just once a day. Just turn on the Change Picture checkbox in the Desktop preferences pane, and choose the amount of time you want between changes from the pop-up menu. When that amount of time goes by, it will change to the next background in that folder. If that becomes too predictable, turn on the Random Order checkbox below it.

Your Own Photos as Desktop Backgrounds

If you want a really custom look for your desktop background, you can choose one of your own photos as your background (instead of using one of Apple's). Go under the Apple menu and choose System Preferences, then click on the Desktop & Screen Saver icon, and when that pane appears, click on the Desktop tab at the top. If you look in the list of folders on the left, you'll notice there are two places Leopard lets you choose photos from: (1) Your Pictures folder (so if you have any photos in there, you're just two clicks away). First, click on the Pictures folder in the list, and then when it displays the photos in your folder, click on the photo you want as your desktop background. (2) If you've created any photo albums in Apple's iPhoto application (see Chapter 8), you can choose a photo from any album. First, click on the little right-facing triangle that appears to the left of iPhoto Albums in the list on the left side, then below it will appear a list of all your albums and imported photo sets. Just click on the album (or set) you want to look at, and the contents of that album will appear to the right (as seen here). Click on the photo you want, and that becomes your desktop background. Now just close the System Preferences dialog by clicking on the round red Close button in the upper-left corner, and you're set.

Put the Dock Where You Want It

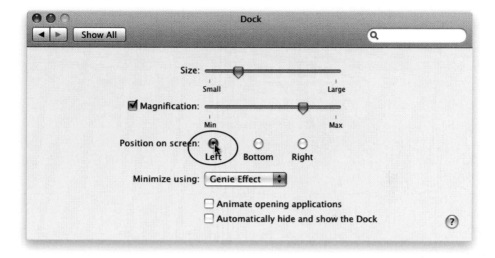

By default, your Dock appears along the bottom of your screen, but if you'd like it on the left or right side of your screen instead, you can change this in the Dock preferences (under the Apple icon, choose System Preferences, then click on the Dock icon). When the Dock preferences pane appears, you'll see you have three choices for where your Dock appears: Left, Bottom, or Right. Click on your choice, then close the dialog by clicking on the round red Close button in the upper-left corner.

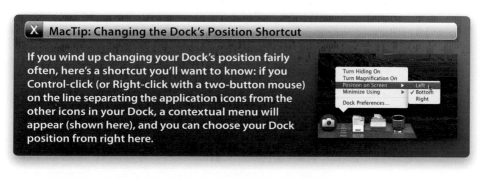

MacTip: Changing the Dock's Position Shortcut

If you wind up changing your Dock's position fairly often, here's a shortcut you'll want to know: if you Control-click (or Right-click with a two-button mouse) on the line separating the application icons from the other icons in your Dock, a contextual menu will appear (shown here), and you can choose your Dock position from right here.

Colorizing Folders

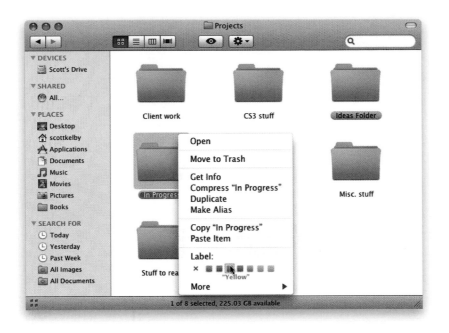

By default, all the folders you create in Leopard look the same (same color, same shape, etc.), but one way you can make a folder stand out (so you can see right where it is at a quick glance) is to add a color label. It doesn't change the color of the folder itself—instead it puts a color fill behind the name of the folder, but it's more effective at catching your eye than this description makes it sound (take a look at the capture above and you'll see what I mean). To apply a label, just Control-click (or if you have a two-button mouse, Right-click) on the folder and then choose your label color from the contextual menu, as shown here. To remove the color, bring up that same contextual menu, but choose the little X at the far left of the colors, and it returns to its default color.

Using Custom Icons

If you'd like to use a custom icon for a folder, it's easy (well, it's easy as long as you have the icon you want to use. If you don't have one you like, you can find about a bazillion for free to download on the Web. Just go to Google.com and search for "Mac OS X icons"). Once you download a custom icon you want to use (they usually download as empty folders), just click on the icon you want to use, then press Command-I (the keys on either side of the Spacebar, plus the letter I) to bring up the Get Info dialog. Up in the top-left corner of that dialog, you'll see a tiny icon. Click once on it and it highlights. Now press Command-C to Copy that icon into memory, and then close that Get Info dialog by clicking on the round red Close button in the upper-left corner. Go to the folder or file where you'd like that custom icon to appear, and click on it. Then press Command-I to bring up its Get Info dialog. Click on its little icon in the upper left (shown circled above), then press Command-V to Paste that icon you copied earlier over the existing icon. Now you can close the Get Info dialog and you're done.

X MacTip: Removing Custom Icons

If you added a custom icon to a document or folder, and later decide you want the original default icon back, just click on it, then press Command-I to bring up the Get Info dialog. Click once on the custom icon up in the top-left corner, then press the Delete key on your keyboard. That's it—your custom icon is gone and is replaced with the original default icon.

Choosing How Big You Want Your Icons

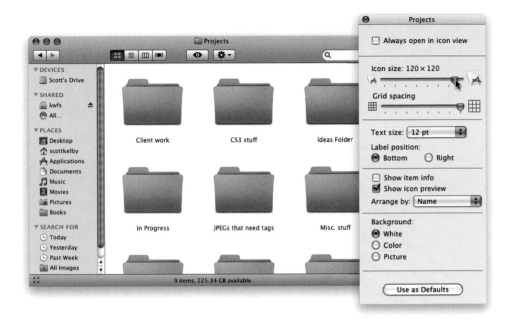

If you bought a large-screen Mac (with a 24" or larger screen), you might feel like the folder and document icons are a little small (by the way, is it just me or as I get older do the icons seem to be getting smaller and smaller? Hey, I'm just sayin'…). Anyway, if they look small to you, you can make them bigger. Much bigger! Just click on any folder, and to make the icons inside that folder larger, press Command-J to bring up the View Options for that folder. You'll see a slider in there for Icon Size (seen above), and as you click-and-drag the slider to the right, the icons resize in real time. A little below that slider is a pop-up menu where you can choose a larger text size for the name of your documents and folders (by the way, if you use either of these, you're probably eligible for special prices at McDonald's. Hey, come on, I'm just kidding. Kinda).

Organizing Your Folders (Loose or Strict?)

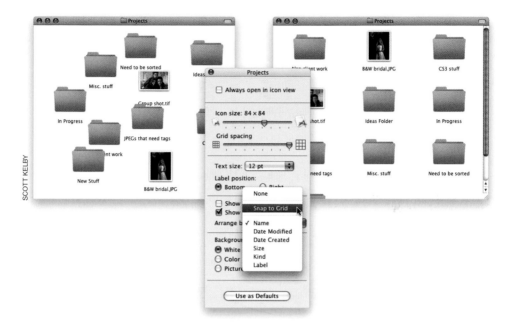

SCOTT KELBY

You get the choice of just how organized you want the contents of your folders to be. By default, in Icon view, there's no real organization scheme—it's kind of a random, messy, leave-'em-where-they-land type of arrangement (shown above left). However, If you prefer that documents and folders inside your folder are neatly arranged into rows, perhaps even sorted alphabetically (shown above right), you can choose that instead (but the one you choose says a lot about your personality, and your therapist may ask you one day which option you chose, so choose carefully). To make your folder world neat and orderly, you have to first open the folder you want to organize, then press Command-J to bring up the View Options for that folder. Then, in the View Options dialog, from the Arrange By pop-up menu, choose Snap to Grid (as shown above) to have the files and folders snap to an invisible grid, which puts them in nice tidy rows. If you'd also like Leopard to alphabetize them for you at the same time, instead choose Name (then they're arranged alphabetically by name). Now, personally I'm not a real organized person by nature (I'm more of a creative type), so you'd think I'd like it "loose and free," but since I'm not naturally organized, I actually like having Leopard do the organizing and alphabetizing for me. Makes ya stop and think, doesn't it? Anyway, if you want to be really Type A, there's a Grid Spacing slider near the top of the View Options dialog that lets you choose how much space appears between the columns of icons (click-and-drag to the right to add space, or to the left for less space).

Seeing More Info on Your Files

If you want to see more than just the filename or folder name in a Finder window, you can turn on the item info, and if Leopard can display more info about the file, it will. This extra info appears directly below the filename (or folder name) in a light blue color, and tells you everything from how many items are in a particular folder, to how long a QuickTime movie is, to the size (in pixels) of a photo. To turn this feature on, open the folder where you want this extra info to appear, and press Command-J to bring up the View Options for that folder. Then turn on the Show Item Info checkbox (as shown here).

See Only What You Want on the Desktop

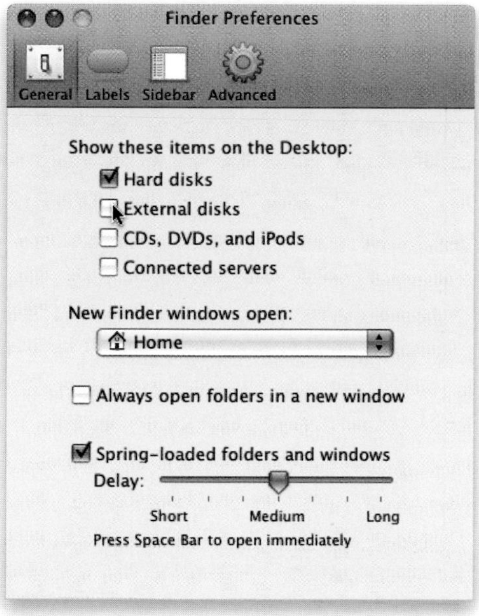

Finder Preferences

General | Labels | Sidebar | Advanced

Show these items on the Desktop:
☑ Hard disks
☐ External disks
☐ CDs, DVDs, and iPods
☐ Connected servers

New Finder windows open:
⌂ Home

☐ Always open folders in a new window

☑ Spring-loaded folders and windows
Delay: ————————————
Short   Medium   Long
Press Space Bar to open immediately

You can control how many external items appear on your desktop—I'm talking things like connected servers, external drives, CDs, DVDs, etc. You'll still have access to all these items right from any Finder window (they'll still appear along the left side of the window), so it's okay to keep them off the desktop, if you like that super-uncluttered look. To choose what appears on the desktop, click on the desktop, and under the Finder menu, choose Preferences. When the Finder Preferences dialog appears (shown above), click on the General icon at the top left, then turn off the checkboxes beside the items you don't want to appear on the desktop. When you're done, just close the dialog by clicking on the round red Close button in the upper-left corner.

See Time Displayed Your Way

The little digital clock that appears up in the top-right corner of your Mac's screen has a surprising number of options for how it displays the time. In fact, you don't even have to view it as a digital clock at all—you can click directly on the digital clock and a menu pops up where you can choose View as Analog, and it then displays your clock as a tiny round analog clock with minute and hour hands like a wristwatch. If you want to take things further, from that same pop-up menu, choose Open Date & Time to open those preferences. From here, click on the Clock tab (up top) and you'll see an entire panel that lets you tweak the layout of your clock in a number of ways, and as you make changes, they're reflected in the digital (or analog) clock itself live as you make them. There's even a preference to have your Mac verbally announce the time each hour. Again, an ideal prank to pull on a co-worker (it'll take 'em 30 minutes to figure out where to turn it off).

Making Everything Bigger

Color LCD

Show All

Display   Color

Resolutions:

720 x 480 (stretched)
800 x 500
800 x 600
800 x 600 (stretched)
1024 x 640
1024 x 768
1024 x 768 (stretched)
1152 x 720
1280 x 800
1440 x 900

Colors: Millions

Refresh Rate: n/a

Detect Displays

☑ Show displays in menu bar   ?

Brightness:

☑ Automatically adjust brightness as ambient light changes

If you'd like to see everything bigger (and I mean everything), you can lower your screen resolution so everything is significantly bigger. To do this, go under the Apple menu and choose System Preferences, then click on the Displays icon. Now, click on the Display tab (up top), and a list of resolutions supported on your Mac will appear on the left side. Your current display resolution will be highlighted, and all you have to do is choose the next smaller size resolution. For example, my MacBook Pro is set at 1440x900, so I'd choose the next smaller size, which is 1280x800 (as shown above). Now everything (my whole screen) is zoomed in closer. So, what's the tradeoff? There are two: (1) your screen is zoomed in closer, so you can fit less on the screen, and (2) the screen will look a little softer, because Macs ship with screens set to their ideal "native" screen resolution, which provides the sharpest, crispest view. So if you choose a non-native view, it's a little softer. Some folks gladly trade size for sharpness, and the only way you'll know is to give it a try and see for yourself.

X MacTip: A Faster Way to Change Resolutions

If you change resolutions fairly often, go to the System Preferences, to the Displays preferences, and turn on the checkbox for Show Displays in Menu Bar. This adds a small display icon at the right side of your menu bar—click-and-hold on it and a pop-up menu of resolutions will appear, so you can choose your resolution right there.

Adding Custom Names for Your Labels

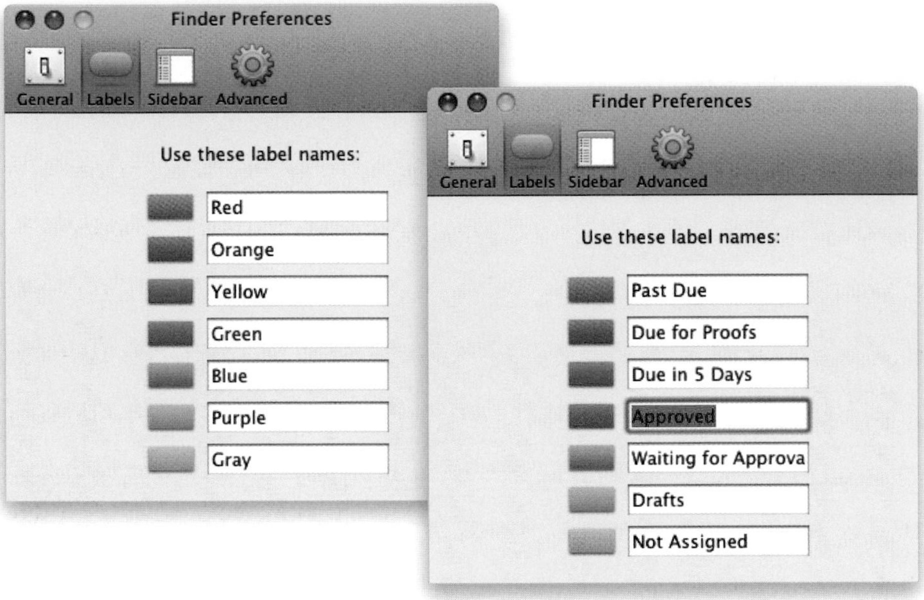

If you're using color labels (to add a color fill to a file's or folder's name to help you find it at a quick glance), you can assign custom names to each color (for your own organizational purposes). Click on the desktop, and under the Finder menu, choose Preferences. When the dialog appears, click on the Labels icon (up top) and the dialog you see above left appears, with the standard color names beside each color (boring!). To add your own custom names, just click-and-drag your cursor over the first name (Red) to highlight it, and type in a new name. Now you can use the Tab key on your keyboard to tab down to the next field, and the text will already be highlighted for you—just type in the name you want, then tab to the next field. When you're done, close the Finder Preferences dialog by clicking on the round red Close button in the upper-left corner. Now, here's the cool thing: when you Control-click on a file (or Right-click, if you have a two-button mouse), and the contextual menu appears where you can assign labels, as you move your cursor over the colors, your custom names will now appear below the colors, so you know which is which. Pretty clever.

Controlling What You See in Your Sidebar

Here's another way to make sure you don't get icon overload, and that's to decide which items you want to appear (or not appear) in the sidebar that appears on the left side of your Finder window. You choose what makes it (and what doesn't) by clicking on the desktop, then going under the Finder menu, and choosing Preferences. When the dialog appears, click on the Sidebar icon up top, then from the list of items that already appear in your sidebar, turn off the checkbox next to the ones you want hidden from view, and voilá—your sidebar has become less cluttered.

Customizing Your Colors

If you want to change the color of your Mac's overall appearance, there's an Appearance preferences pane where you can choose a different color (don't get too excited—it's a pretty subtle change, and you only get two choices—Blue or Graphite—as shown above), and while you're in this pane, you can also choose a number of other customization settings, including how many items appear in your Recent Items list (the Recent Items menu lets you get back quickly to applications, documents, or servers you've used recently, without digging through a bunch of menus—you just go under the Apple menu and choose them directly from the Recent Items submenu). There are also two controls for what happens when you click in the scroll bar, and you can choose whether you want the scroll bar arrows (which move the scroll bar each time you click on them, without you clicking-and-dragging the bar itself) at the top and bottom of each scroll bar, or together at the bottom (the advantage of putting them at the bottom is they're both right there, so there's less scrolling—especially if you go just past where you wanted to be—you don't have to go all the way up [or down] to get to the other arrow). There's another important control: the highlight color, and it's so important, it gets its own page (that's coming up next).

Changing Your Highlight Color

When I get a new Mac, one of the first things I do is change the highlight color (the color things change to when you click on them). That's because I've always felt that the default highlight color didn't stand out enough, and sometimes I'd be in a list and it wasn't instantly obvious when a file was selected, because the default color is kind of a light blue. So, I go to the System Preferences (under the Apple menu), click on Appearance (the pane is shown on the previous page), and choose Gold from the Highlight Color pop-up menu. This is why, throughout this book, anytime something's highlighted (even in a text field), it always appears in gold. I wanted it to be easier for you to see. So, if it's easier to see here in the book, why not make it easier to see in person by following the steps I just outlined? Above (top left), I show what it looks like when a folder is selected with Gold as the highlight color. Below that is the folder name highlighted, and then to the right of those is an Open dialog, and you can see how the folder I selected stands out in gold. It takes two seconds, and it sure makes selected items really stand out.

Picking a Screen Saver

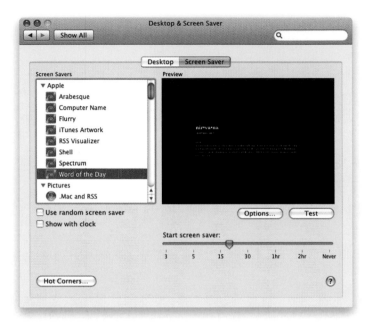

Your Mac has a screen saver built right in (hey, I remember back to the days where we had to buy a screen saver separately). This puppy kicks in after a few minutes of inactivity, and there was a time when screen savers were absolutely necessary to keep the current image onscreen from burning permanently onto your screen (remember those days? Gas was cheap, but our screens burned in. It's always something, isn't it?). Anyway, today's screens are so advanced they no longer require a screen saver that's moving all the time…but apparently we do. Of course, everybody wants to choose a special one that reflects their unique, special, one-of-a-kind individuality, and you can choose from any one of the built-in screen savers (used by untold millions of unique, special, one-of-a-kind individuals like yourself) by going under the Apple menu and choosing System Preferences. Then click on the Desktop & Screen Saver icon, and last click on the Screen Saver tab up top to reveal the list of screen savers. On the left, are the ones provided by Apple. If the one you've chosen has customizable options, you'll see an Options button below the Preview window—if you click it, any preferences for that screen saver will appear in a separate dialog. Below Apple's screen savers, you have access to your Pictures folder (so you can have slowly moving photos as your screen saver), or you can chose an album or set of photos in iPhoto (and they'll move slowly, as well). To see a preview of any of them, click on one, then press the Test button. You choose how much time passes before it takes over your screen using the slider on the lower right.

Choosing Your Alert Sound

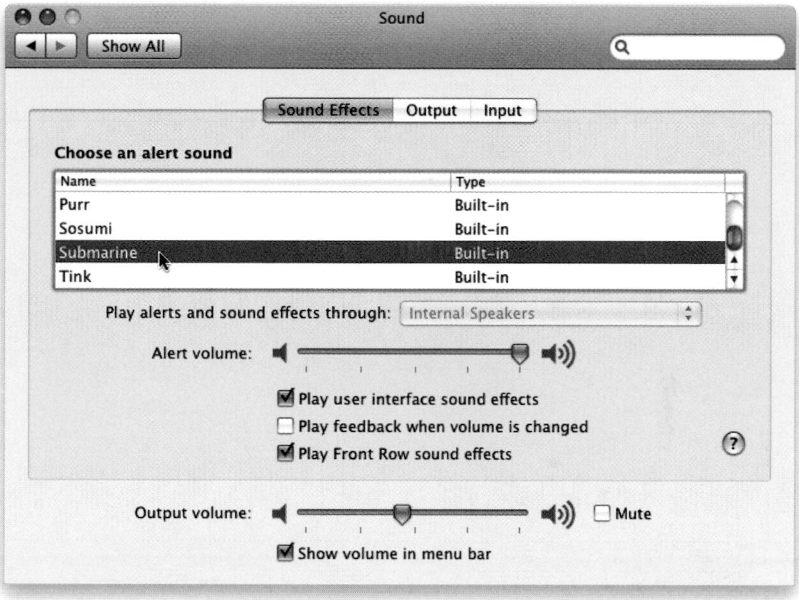

When you do something (anything) that your Mac doesn't want you to do, it gives you an alert sound. After a while, that alert sound starts to get on your nerves because each time you hear it, you know you're "messing up." Now, I've found it's easier to change the alert sound than it is to stop messing up, so if you want to change your alert sound to a less irritating sound, go under the Apple menu and choose System Preferences, then click on the Sound icon. When the Sound pane appears, click on the Sound Effects tab up top (as shown here) and then you'll see a list of the built-in alert sounds you can choose from. If you click on any sound, it plays a preview of the sound, so you can try them out and find out which one sends the least chills up your spine. You can also control the volume of your alert sound using the Alert Volume slider right below the list. Once you've found one you like, click on it, then close the dialog by clicking on the round red Close button in the upper-left corner.

Adding Your Photo to Your Address Book

The Address Book application on your Mac does more than just track addresses. It's the heart of so many different parts of your Mac experience that even if you don't want to use it for storing your addresses, I still recommend that you at least add one address in the address book—yours. That's because, once you do (and add your photo to it, which is key), your Mac will automatically put that photo in really handy places. For example, if you go to do an iChat, it automatically grabs that photo from your Address Book and uses it as your chat avatar, so when you're chatting with another Mac user, they see your face. This is just one instance, but there are many more, so it's definitely worth doing. To do this, go to the Dock and launch the Address Book application. Then click the little + (plus sign) button below the second column and a new address card appears, where you can type in your information (the name field is already highlighted, so just type it right in, then use the Tab key on your keyboard to jump from field to field). Once your personal info is in place, find a photo of you on your Mac, then click-and-drag it right onto that little empty photo square that appears to the left of your name, and let go of the mouse. This brings up a photo editor window (shown above), where you can use the slider to resize the photo and you can click-and-drag the photo to reposition it, as you'd like. When you're done, click the Set button, and you're all set—your photo is included in your Address Book, your iChats, and anywhere you need it fast.

No Photo Handy? Use Your Mac's Camera

If you don't have a photo of yourself that's suitable for using in Address Book, then have your Mac take one for you. All new Mac laptops and iMacs have built-in cameras right on the display, and it's perfect for taking your photo for Address Book. Here's how: when you're in Address Book and you're creating your new address card (in the Edit mode), just double-click directly on that square photo area to the left of where your name is, and the edit window shows up, and at the bottom of this window is a camera button. Click that, and it turns on the built-in camera on your Mac, and shows you a preview of…well…you! It gives you a 3-2-1 visual countdown, then your whole screen flashes once (like the flash of a camera) and your photo appears in the window for you to resize (using the slider) and position (click-and-drag it). To the right of the camera button is a special effects button, and clicking it will bring up a window displaying your photo with various special effects applied to it. Some are cool, but some are very cruel and should only be used on photos of friends, not your own. There are six panels of these effects, with a thumbnail of each, and if you decide not to use one (one can only hope), go back to the first panel and click on the thumbnail named "Original." Then click the Set button, and you're set!

Creating a Custom Login Photo

SCOTT KELBY

If you are on a Mac with multiple users, or it's just you, but someone else administers your Mac (meaning someone maintains it, adds applications, configures it, etc., so they have a special "I can mess with that kind of stuff" account), then you have to log in each time with a username and password. Your Administrator may have chosen one of Apple's built-in icons to represent you, or when you first bought your Mac, you may have chosen one, because if you're new to the Mac, you probably didn't have a good photo handy—most folks (at this new stage) don't take up Apple's offer to use their built-in camera to take a photo the first time they start their Mac. So, all this time, you've been stuck with that darn icon of a butterfly (or worse) as your login icon. Well, it's time to set up your own custom login photo. Here's how: In Finder, go to your Applications folder and double-click on Photo Booth (providing, of course, that you're using a new Mac laptop or an iMac, both of which have a built-in camera). When it appears, you can choose from having it take one photo (as I did above), a quick series of four photos, or a movie clip by clicking on one of the buttons on the left. Choose either one or four, then sit back and strike a pose (you'll see a live onscreen preview). Click on the Shutter button (the red button with the camera icon) in the middle and once your photo appears in the filmstrip along the bottom, you can click on it to see a larger version. Click the Account Picture button (as shown above), and it opens the Accounts preferences dialog and puts the photo in there for you. If you click on your photo and choose Edit Picture, it brings up the same photo editor you get for Address Book (see the previous pages), so you can resize and position the photo as you'd like.

48

Choosing When Your Mac Goes to Sleep

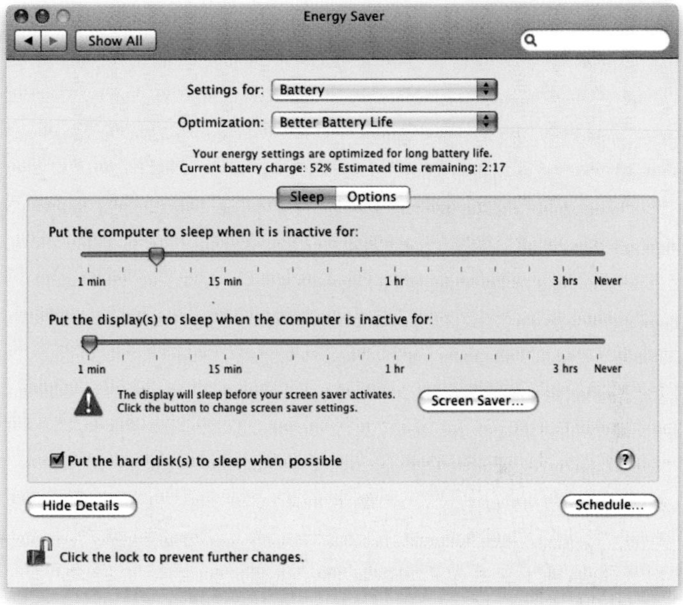

If you've been working on your Mac, and you walk away to take a break, or do some light shoplifting, etc., your Mac will go to sleep to conserve energy (if you're plugged in) or battery power (if you're not), and your screen will sleep, as well, to conserve its life. This is a good thing, and luckily your Mac wakes from its slumber as soon as you press any key, move the mouse, or click the trackpad button. Although it's preset to go to sleep at a certain interval at the factory, you can choose exactly how long you want it to remain awake before it goes to sleep (if ever). Here's how: Go under the Apple menu and choose System Preferences, then click on the Energy Saver icon. You get to choose separate settings for when your Mac is running on battery power (as seen above), or when it's plugged in. Click on the Sleep tab, and then you can use the sliders to choose how long before your inactive Mac goes to sleep. There's a separate slider in case you want the display to go to sleep sooner than the computer (a big battery saver!). When you're done, just click the round red Close button in the upper-left corner.

Changing the Speed of Your Mouse

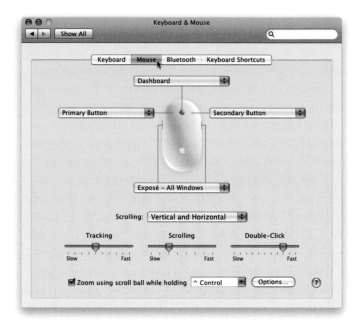

You can totally control the speed your mouse moves (well, it's actually the speed of your cursor onscreen, right?) by going under the Apple menu and choosing System Preferences, then clicking on the Keyboard & Mouse icon. When that pane appears, click on the Mouse tab (as shown above) to bring up the Mouse preferences. The Tracking slider controls how fast your cursor is going to move as you move the mouse. On the right, the Double-Click slider tells your Mac how fast (or slow) you double-click, so it can distinguish between a double-click and two separate clicks. If you're a fast double-clicker (and you know who you are), then click-and-drag the slider to the right. If you're slower, and more deliberate, then click-and-drag the slider to the left. If you have a two-button mouse, you can also choose the speed windows (and webpages) scroll when using the scroll ball by clicking-and-dragging the Scrolling slider. When you're done making your tweaks, close the dialog by clicking on the round red Close button in the upper-left corner.

Changing the Speed of Your Trackpad

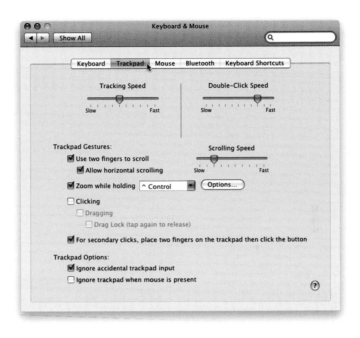

If you're using a MacBook, a MacBook Pro, or a MacBook Air, you can control how fast your cursor moves when using the trackpad. Go under the Apple menu and choose System Preferences, then click on the Keyboard & Mouse icon. When that pane appears, click on the Trackpad tab (as shown above) to bring up the Trackpad preferences. The Tracking Speed slider controls how fast your cursor is going to move as you move your finger on the trackpad. To the right of that, the Double-Click Speed slider tells your Mac how fast (or slow) you double-click, so it can distinguish between a double-click and two separate clicks. If you're a fast double-clicker, then click-and-drag the slider to the right. If you're slower, and more deliberate, then click-and-drag the slider to the left. You can also scroll windows (and webpages) by placing two fingers on the trackpad, and dragging up/down or side to side, and the speed you scroll is controlled by the Scrolling Speed slider. When you're done making your tweaks, close the dialog by clicking on the round red Close button in the upper-left corner.

Choosing What's in Your Dock

By default, Apple puts the programs in your Dock that you're most likely to use, but as you install additional applications, or find that you don't use certain applications, you'll probably want to customize the Dock your way. To remove an icon from the Dock, just click on it and drag it up and away from the Dock and a little puff of smoke will appear (as shown above) to let you know it's gone. If you want to add an application to the Dock, just go to the Applications folder, and click-and-drag the application's icon right onto the Dock and it stays put. Easy enough. If you want to change the order of items in the Dock, just click on 'em and drag 'em where you want 'em.

X MacTip: Keeping a Running Application in the Dock

If you installed a new program (or downloaded it from the Web), and you realize that you'll be using it a lot, you might want to keep it in your Dock for easy one-click access. To do that, while the application is running, just Control-click (or Right-click) on its icon in the Dock, and from the contextual menu that appears, choose Keep in Dock.

Clearing the Clutter (Setting Up Spaces)

If your work area feels like it's getting cluttered, and you're constantly moving or hiding other applications, you need space. Actually, you need Spaces, which is a very cool feature of Leopard that lets you arrange things just the way you want, with minimal clutter, when you're working in your favorite applications or projects. For example, if you don't want any distractions when you're reading your mail, you can set up a Mail Space, where all that's visible is your Mail application, and everything else is hidden. You still have access to everything, but by default, it's all hidden. Here's how to set up your own custom Spaces. Go under the Apple menu and choose System Preferences, then click on Exposé & Spaces, then click on the Spaces tab up top. You can have lots of different spaces, but for now, let's just use the default number of four. Click the little + (plus sign) button (as shown above) to add an application that you want to have its own Space. This brings up a standard Open dialog, so choose an application you use often (for the sake of our example, I'll choose Mail), then click the Add button. Your application now appears in the Application Assignments list. To the right of that list, under the Space column, click-and-hold and choose Space 1 from the pop-up menu. Now do the same thing for the other applications you use daily, but assign each one to a different numbered space (2, 3, and 4—you can add more spaces later if you want), then close the dialog by clicking on the round red Close button in the upper-left corner. On the next page, you'll see how to put Spaces to work.

Using Spaces

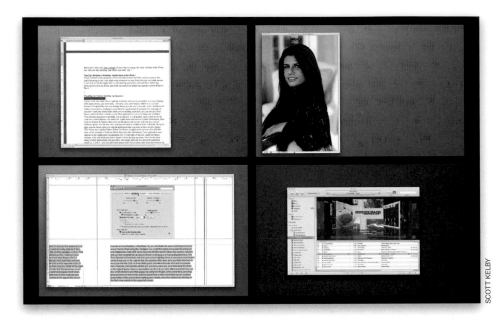

SCOTT KELBY

Now that you have four applications assigned to four different spaces, let's try them out. First, press the F8 key on your keyboard (Fn-F8 on a laptop; this is the shortcut to activate Spaces), and your screen changes to display four large windows, each one with an application in it. To jump to any application, just click on it, and you now see just that application and all the others are hidden from view (except the desktop, of course). Anytime you want to switch to another uncluttered space, just press F8, then click on the one you want. You can also press-and-hold the Control key and use the Arrow keys on your keyboard to move between Spaces.

X MacTip: Add Spaces to Your Menu Bar

If you'd prefer direct access to your Spaces, right from your menu bar up top (rather than using the F8 shortcut), go back to the Spaces preferences and turn on the checkbox for Show Spaces in Menu Bar. This adds a little square number, and if you click on it, a list pops up with all your Space choices, and one-click access to the Spaces preferences.

Turning Off Menu Transparency

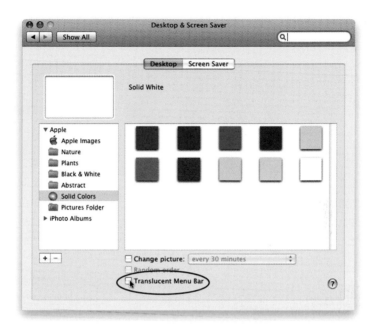

One of the things that drove a lot of people crazy when Leopard first shipped was that the menu bar (that appears at the top of, well…everything) was transparent. Luckily, not long after Leopard first shipped, Apple made the transparency an option (so you could choose to have a solid menu bar instead, like in all previous versions of the Mac OS). To turn off this transparency, go under the Apple menu and choose System Preferences. Click on the Desktop & Screen Saver icon, then click on the Desktop tab. At the bottom of this pane, turn off the checkbox for Translucent Menu Bar and close the System Preferences by clicking on the round red Close button at the top left of the dialog. That's it—you're back to a solid menu bar. Ahhhhh, that's better.

Get to Your Stuff Quicker Using Stacks

Although the main job of the Dock is to give you one-click access to some of your applications, it has another related gig, and that is to give you two-click access to all of the things you download from the Web and all your documents (you can also add any folder you want, like your Applications folder, as I did here. See the tip at the bottom of the next page for how to do this). That's what those folders are that you see at the far-right side of the Dock here. Since Apple knows you'll most likely be using those folders a lot, they put aliases (pointers) to them right there, so you can get to their contents any time you'd like using a feature Apple calls "stacks." Here's why stacks are so helpful: Let's say you want to launch an application that's not already in your Dock; you'd have to go to Finder, go to your Applications folder, open it, find the application, and launch it. That just takes too long—instead, just click once on the Applications stack (if you added it to the far-right side of your Dock, like I did) and a window pops up (shown above) displaying the contents of that folder, so you can just click on what you want to launch. No having to go to Finder, or navigating through folders—it's right there all the time. If you download something from the Web, you're just one click away from that, too—just click on the Downloads folder in the Dock, and everything you've downloaded is displayed onscreen. The window and icons automatically resize, so you can see everything. It's really amazingly handy (try it once—you'll be hooked). You can also choose how your stacks are displayed, but I cover that on the next page.

Choosing How Your Stacks Look

There are three different "looks" to stacks, and you get to choose the one you like the best. The Grid view is the one you see on the previous page, where it pops up in a semi-transparent window, but there are two other looks as well: (1) a Fan view, where the most recent items pop up in a fan-like arc (see above left) and if you want to see the rest of what's in that folder, you'd click the More in Finder button at the top of the fan; and (2) a List view, where what's inside the folder shows up in a regular pop-up menu (as seen above center). You get to choose which of these three views you want (or you can have your Mac choose which of the three it thinks is best based on how many items are in the folder, using its Automatic view) by pressing-and-holding the Control key and clicking (or Right-clicking) on any one of those stacking folders. A contextual menu (shown top right) appears, where you can make your choice for how you want your stacks to look.

X MacTip: You Can Add Your Own Stacks

If you want to add one of your own folders as a stack in the Dock—no sweat—just drag-and-drop the folder directly onto the right end of the Dock, and it automatically becomes a stack. If there's a default folder you find you don't use, you can just click-and-drag it right out of the Dock. To change the order of your folder stacks, just click-and-drag them.

Having Two People Use the Same Mac

Let's say you bought two Macs—one for you and one for your child. Your Macs would probably look very different, right? (Well, at least my son's and mine do.) He's got an Xbox 360 Halo 3 desktop background, and he likes his Dock on the side of the screen, and he uses a totally different set of applications than I do, and well...let's just say his Mac looks a lot different than my Mac, and that's to be expected—two different Macs; two different personalities. Now, what's really cool is you can have this same experience on one single Mac—where multiple people work and play on the same Mac. Each can have their own separate desktop background and applications, and set up their Mac their way. You do this by setting up a separate account for each user, and when you're done working on the Mac, you log out, and your child (or spouse, co-worker, etc.) signs in and they only see their setup, look, and feel—they have no access to your stuff. It's like having two separate Macs. To set up separate accounts, go under the Apple menu and choose System Preferences. When the Preferences dialog appears, click on Accounts (it's in the fourth row under System). When the Accounts preferences appear, click on the little + (plus sign) button in the bottom-left corner of the pane to add a new account (it may prompt you for your password). If the + is grayed out, click the Lock icon beneath it, which will definitely prompt you for your password, but will then allow you to create new accounts. A dialog will pop down where you enter your second user's account info (in this case, I'm sharing my Mac with my book editor, Kim Doty). Just choose a user-name, password, etc., and click the Create Account Button.

Switching Between Two (or More) Users

Once you've set up multiple accounts (as shown on the previous page), you have two choices when you're done working on your Mac: (1) You can go under the Apple menu and choose Log Out. This quits all your applications, so when you log back on, you'll need to re-launch any applications to get back to work. Or (2) you can use Fast User Switching, where you leave your work as is (with your documents and applications still open), and when another person logs in, the screen just "flips over," so now they're working on their version of the Mac (the flipping effect is pretty cool, by the way). To do the "flips over" thing, you have to turn it on, and to do that, go back to the Accounts preferences (the same place where you created your new account), and click on the Login Options button (it's at the bottom of the list of accounts on the left. It has a house icon on it). When the Login Options appear, turn on the Enable Fast User Switching checkbox, which adds a pop-up menu to the top-right corner of your screen, with your username and anyone else's name that has an account on the Mac. To switch between them, just choose a name from this pop-up menu and it flips over to their look, feel, applications, etc., just like you were switching Macs. When you switch back to your account, all your applications, documents, etc., will be right where you left them (kind of like you just put your Mac to sleep). By the way, if one person uses this Mac the most, you can have it automatically log in this person each time the Mac is turned on by choosing their username from the Automatic Login pop-up menu at the top of the Login Options pane.

More Tips for Customizing Your Mac

X MacTip: Hiding Your Top Toolbar and Sidebar

If you want to hide the toolbar across the top, and the sidebar along the left side of any Finder window, just press Command-Option-T.

X MacTip: You Can Use the Sidebar Like the Dock

If you find yourself using one particular application a lot, you can drag-and-drop that application's icon right into the sidebar of any Finder window, and now that application will be just one click away, from now on. To remove it from the sidebar, just click-and-drag the icon right off of it.

X MacTip: Changing the Order of Your Columns in a Finder Window

When you're looking at a window in List view, by default it displays with the Name column first, then Date Modified, then Size, etc., but if you'd like the Size first, or Date Modified first, you can just drag-and-drop the columns into the order you'd like them.

X MacTip: Jumping Between Finder Window Views

You can jump between the various window views (Icon view, List view, Column view, and Cover Flow), by pressing Command-1, Command-2, Command-3, and so on.

X MacTip: Moving Icons Anywhere You Want Them

In Icon view, if you have Snap to Grid turned on (so your icons in your Finder window stay nicely organized in rows and columns), but you want to move an icon to a spot that isn't in line with a row or column, just press-and-hold the Command key and drag the file where you want it.

More Tips for Customizing Your Mac

X MacTip: Three Ways to Eject CDs, DVDs, or External Hard Drives

Click on the disc/disk in Finder's sidebar, and then either: (1) click on the Eject button that appears to its right; (2) click-and-drag the disc/disk to the Trash icon on the Dock; (3) click on the disc/disk and press Command-E; (4) click on the disc/disk, go under the File menu, and choose Eject; or (5) Control-click (or Right-click) on the disc/disk on the desktop and choose Eject from the contextual menu.

X MacTip: Empty the Trash from the Trash

If you want to quickly empty the Trash, just Control-click (or Right-click) on the Trash icon in the Dock, and choose Empty Trash from the contextual menu.

X MacTip: Rearranging the Menu Bar Icons

If you want to change the order of the icons in the right side of your Mac's menu bar, just press-and-hold the Command key, and click-and-drag the icons where you'd like them. To remove an icon from the menu bar, press-and-hold the same key, but then click-and-drag the icon straight down off the menu bar.

X MacTip: Duplicating Files or Folders

To duplicate a file or folder, press Command-D. You can also press-and-hold the Option key, click on the file, and drag yourself out a copy.

X MacTip: Using Photoshop Thumbnails as Custom Icons

If you use Adobe Photoshop, you'll notice that by default when you save a photo, it creates an icon that is a tiny thumbnail of the photo. You can use any one of those thumbnails as a custom icon to replace a default icon. For example, if you have a shot of your kids, you can copy-and-paste that icon onto the folder where you keep all your family photos.

Chapter Three

Getting Your Life Organized
Getting Your Contacts, Calendars, and Other Stuff Set Up

I think for a lot of people, the reason they want a Mac in the first place is to get their life organized. They have important addresses and phone numbers saved on Post-it notes and little slips of paper, and scribbled on the back of their own business cards, and the idea of having all this information right at their fingertips is really appealing. That's why my dad got his first Mac. He used to carry around a Franklin planner, and his whole life was in that planner—from the names and phone numbers of his doctors, to his calendar, to his credit card numbers, and even a draft of his will. He carried that handwritten planner with him everywhere he went, and he left it, by accident, in approximately 43% of those places on a daily basis. After a while, different restaurants he frequented learned to forward his planner to the next location listed on his calendar, and sometimes it would even beat him there. This worked pretty well most of the time, but sometimes the people who found it would use his credit card numbers to buy things online, and then when he got the bill, he couldn't remember if he actually ordered those things, because (you guessed it) he had misplaced his planner. So, for his birthday one year we got him an iMac, and we set up his calendar, and his address book, and set up his first email account, and meticulously typed in all his handwritten notes, and generally brought him out of the Stone Age, and he seemed pretty happy, until one day my dad, my brother, and I were out to lunch and a guy walked in carrying my dad's 20" iMac and said, "You left this in your golf cart at the pro shop." We all laughed, and loaded his iMac into the car. Dad must have been really impressed with that guy's gesture that day though, because when he passed away, he left him nearly all of his estate. My dad—he was some character.

Managing Your Contacts

This is going to sound like I'm exaggerating at first, but if you use your Mac's Address Book for managing your content, it will make your whole Mac experience better, easier, and more efficient. You'll have to trust me on this for now, but as you go through the book, it will totally make sense. So, start by launching Address Book (it's in the Dock or in your Applications folder), and when you launch it for the first time, there's only one address in your Address Book—Apple's. (The bonus is: the phone number works.) The process is pretty simple from here: you're going to add contacts on the right side (more on this in the following pages), then later create groups (kind of like folders) to help keep your contacts organized and get you to the right people quickly. Don't be fooled by its simple interface, Address Book is much more than it appears, and it's super-fast, easy to set up, easy to use, and pretty darn clever at managing your contacts and working with the rest of your Mac (and your iPhone and/or iPod if you've got one or both). So, that's the scoop. Let's get to it.

Add Yourself First. This Is Important

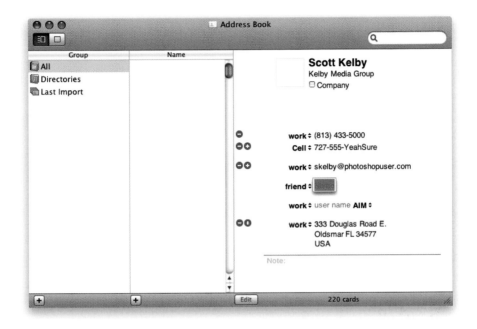

The first thing you've got to do is to add you, and your full contact info, to the Address Book (this is a key part of that whole making-your-experience-better-and-easier thing), so click on the + (plus sign) button at the bottom of the Name column, and it creates a new blank card. Just type in your first name and tab to the next field, and basically just tab around and enter your full and complete contact info (yes, you really have to do this). If you need to add extra phone or email fields, just click the green + (plus sign) button to the left of the field you want to add. To remove a field, click the red – (minus sign) button. When you're done, click on the Edit button below your card and your card is saved. Then (and this is very important), go up under the Card menu and choose Make This My Card. I know, it seems silly, but now your Mac knows exactly who you are, where you live, your phone number, and it can access this info when it needs it to make your life easier.

X **MacTip: Don't Type Dashes When Entering Phone Numbers**

When you're typing numbers in the phone number field, your Mac knows it's a phone number (after all—it's the phone number field), so you don't have to put in any dashes—just put in a space, and Address Book will automatically put parenthesis around your area code and add the dashes in for you.

Create Your Own Contact Template

Before you start entering all your other contacts, if you know now that you might need more email fields or phone fields, or if you need to include your contact's title and/or department, you might want to create your own custom Address Book template now, with all those fields already in place. You do that by going under the Address Book menu and choosing Preferences. When the Preferences dialog appears, click on the Template icon to bring up the Template preferences. To add a new field that's not already there, choose it from the Add Field pop-up menu in the top-left corner (as shown here) and it adds that field. If you change your mind and want this new field removed, just choose it again in the menu, and it's removed. You learned how to add more phone and email fields on the previous page, so add 'em if you need 'em. When you're done tweaking your template, press Command-W to close the Preferences dialog and save your template. From now on, when you create a new contact, it will have all the fields you just added or deleted.

X MacTip: Customize Your Field Names

The field for your wireless phone is called "mobile" by default, but if you call it something else (I call them "cell" phones), you can change the name of that field by clicking on its name and choosing Custom (it's at the bottom of the menu). This brings up the Add Custom Label dialog—just type in the name you'd prefer and click OK.

Getting Contacts into Your Address Book

```
Resent-From:  macgroup-announcements@mail-list.com
      From:  Terry White <terry@terrysmail.com>
   Subject:  You've got MacNews! March issue now available...
      Date:  March 15, 2008 5:20:55 PM EDT
        To:  Scott
```

Hello,
The March issue of Ma
http://www.macgroup.c

Special thanks goes o
Mary Jo Disler
Chita Hunter

Just a reminder that we
Photoshop Elements 6

For meeting details, lo
http://macgroup.org
http://macgroup.org/m

The afterglow will be a
Seros Restaurant
29221 Northwestern H
Southfield, MI 48034
(248) 358-2353

Meeting notes from the February meeting:
http://macgroup.org/meetings/notes_archive/notes_2008/02_17/

See you all tomorrow!

Seros Restaurant
☑ Company

work ⏷   (248) 358-2353
work ⏷   macgroup-announcements-on@mail-list.com
work ⏷   AIM **AIM** ⏷
home ⏷   29221 Northwestern Hwy
         Southfield MI 48034
         Country

[Cancel]   [Add to Address Book]

5th (3-5PM). The meeting topic is the all NEW Adobe cool prizes.

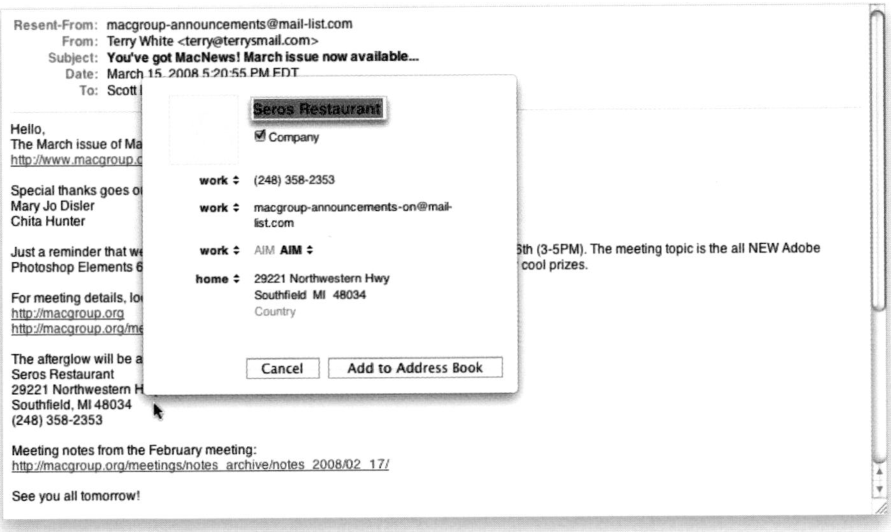

You've already learned how to manually add contacts to your Address Book (you click that + [plus sign] button, and then type in the information, tabbing from field to field), but there are other ways to get contacts into your Address Book (including importing them from other applications and other computers—see the tip at the bottom of this page). Since a lot of our contacts come to us in emails (including within people's signatures), you'll want to know this great technique for taking info in an email straight into your Address Book. When you're reading an email (in Mail) with contact info in it, just move your cursor over any part of that contact info (the address, phone number, etc.) and a gray dotted line will appear around at least part of it with a little arrow. Click on that arrow, and choose Create New Contact from the pop-up menu. A window will appear (shown above) giving you a preview of how it will look in your Address Book. Click the Add to Address Book button, and it does the rest.

X MacTip: Importing Contacts from Other Applications

If you've been using another program to manage your contacts (maybe Entourage, or Outlook in Windows, or Palm software, etc.), you can export those contacts (saving them in a tab-delimited, vCard, comma-separated, or LDIF format), and then you can import them right into your Mac's Address Book by going under the File menu, under Import, and then choosing the type of file to import. A standard Open dialog will appear, asking you to locate the file to import. Click on the file, then click Open to begin the import.

Searching for People in Your Address Book

Once you've entered a number of contacts into your Address Book, you'll see a scrolling list in the center column of all their names. If you only have 20 or 30 people in your list, you're not even going to have to use the search field (in the upper-right corner) to find people—you'll just look for them in the list. To make finding them easier, go under the Address Book menu and choose Preferences. When the Preferences dialog appears, click on the General icon up top, and at the top of the pane that appears, you can choose whether you want first names to appear first or last, and how you want your names sorted (by first name or last name), as shown above. If you do wind up having 50 or more contacts, then it is faster to use the search field. As soon as you start typing even one letter, it starts searching, and the more letters you type, the quicker it gets to your contact (using a very quick process of elimination), and then it only displays the results in the center column. If it only finds one matching contact, that's all it will display.

X MacTip: Changing to a Cleaner, Uncluttered View

The regular view is fine when you're entering new contacts, but once you've added all your contacts, you might prefer a more streamlined, uncluttered look. To see that view, click on the button on the right with a square on it in the top-left corner of the Address Book window. This hides the first two columns and just displays the card. Perfect if you usually use the search field to find your contacts.

Getting More Organized by Using Groups

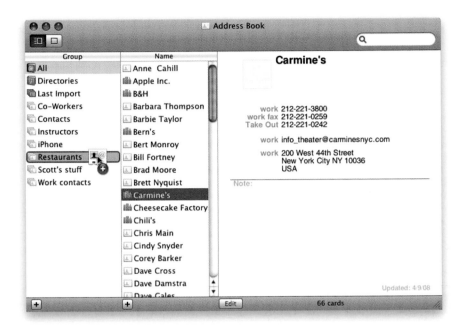

Chances are your Address Book now has a wide range of people and places—everything from business contacts, to friends, to family members, to favorite restaurants, to local businesses, to co-workers. The problem is they're all lumped in there together. That's why groups are so great for getting organized, because you can create groups for all those different collections of people and places, and then you can see just those people and places with one click. That way, if you want to call a restaurant for takeout, you could click on your Restaurants group, and only restaurants would appear in the Name column. To create a group, just click the + (plus sign) button at the bottom-left corner of the first column. This adds an empty group to the column, and its name is highlighted already for you to type in a name (so do that now). Then, just click-and-drag names from the Name column onto that group name. To see all your contact names again, just click on the All group at the top of the first column. Another benefit of groups is when you click on a group, the search field only searches within that group.

❌ MacTip: Editing an Existing Contact

To edit an existing contact (let's say their phone number, extension, or email address changed), just find the contact, then click the Edit button at the bottom-left corner of the card. Make your changes by clicking on the field that needs editing, and when you're done, just click on the Edit button again to save your changes.

Use Smart Groups to Organize Automatically

Address Book

Smart Group Name: Co-Workers

Contains cards which match the following:

Company | is | Kelby Media Group

☑ Highlight group when updated   Cancel   OK

All
Director
Last Imp
Co-Worl
Contacts
Instructc
iPhone
Restaurants
Scott's stuff
Work contacts

Jack Davis
Jack Dennis
Jack Lee
Jack Resnicki
Jason Scrivner
Jay Nelson
Jean A Kendra
Jeff Foster
Jeff Kelby
Jeff Revell
Jeff Sacilotto
Jeff Schewe

home 1735-B Defoor Place NW
Atlanta GA 30318

Note:

Updated: 3/16/08

Edit   220 cards

If you don't feel like manually organizing your contacts into groups, you can have Address Book do it for you using Smart Groups, which automatically group contacts together that share a trait you choose. For example, if you wanted to create a Smart Group for all your co-workers, it keeps an eye on the Company field in every contact, and if it sees your company's name, it puts that contact into your Co-Workers group for you. Each time you add a new co-worker's contact info, the Smart Group automatically adds them, as well. If you change a contact to reflect that they don't work for your company anymore, it removes them. To build your own Smart Group, go under the File menu and choose New Smart Group, which pops down the dialog you see above. Give your Smart Group a name, then from the pop-up menus below, choose the criteria you want your Smart Group to match. In this example, I set the first field to Company, in the second field I chose is, and then in the name field I typed in my company's name. If you want to add more levels of criteria (you could add a second level sorted by departments), just click the + (plus sign) button to the right of the text field (shown circled in red above). When you're done, click OK, and your Smart Group will be assembled automatically. Remember: Smart Groups are live, so as you enter new contacts or edit old ones, they'll automatically be added to (or subtracted from, depending on the criteria you chose) your Smart Groups.

Using Your Mac's Calendar

All the organization tools on your Mac tie into each other, and I just can't stress enough how much easier things will be if you use the whole shebang (namely, Address Book, Mail, and iCal). One of the slickest things about iCal is how you can create different calendars for different things (like one calendar for work, one for home, one for your favorite NFL team's schedule, one for priority items, etc.), and then not only color code them (so you can see at a glance if an item on your calendar is personal or work related), but you can hide these calendars, so with just a click or two, you can see the month with only your home commitments, or only your work commitments, or only your travel schedule. This really brings some perspective and order to your month (year, etc.). So, that being said, let's fire up iCal (it's in the Dock—give it a click). When iCal opens, it opens in the weekly view (showing you the current week) with today's date highlighted. You can view your calendar in this Week view, you can view one day at a time, or you can back out to view the entire month (there's not a right or wrong way—it's just what you prefer).

X MacTip: Jump to Today with One Click

When you're looking through your calendar, anytime you want to jump directly to today's date, you can either click the Today button up in the top-left corner of the iCal window, or just press Command-T, which is the shortcut.

Adding Something to Your Calendar (Month)

Let's start in Month view, so click on the Month button at the top of the iCal window. To add an event to your calendar (like a reminder to call someone, for example), double-click on the day you want to add it to (you can move through the different months using the left and right arrow buttons at the top center of the iCal window, or you can jump directly to a particular day by pressing Command-Shift-T, which brings up a Go to Date dialog, where you can choose the date to want to jump to). When you double-click on a day, it adds a note (called an "event") on that day, and it's already highlighted so you can type in "Call Lisa in Accounting" and then hit the Return key. Now, when you add an event in the Month view like this, it puts a default time for your event. If you actually need to call Lisa at that time, you're in luck. If not, and you need to schedule that call to Lisa at a different time, click on your event, then press Command-E to bring up the Event Editor (shown above). Click directly on the time you want to change to select it, and then just type in the correct time (here, I clicked on the hour and typed in 10, clicked on the minutes and typed in 30, clicked on PM and typed AM, then I pressed the Return key to lock in my changes). Click the Done button when you're finished, and now if you were to view this day in the Day or Week view, you'd see this event has been added to your calendar at exactly 10:30 a.m.

Adding to Your Day/Week View Calendar

If you're adding an event in Day or Week view, you can save yourself some time and, instead, double-click in the calendar on the time that your event is to be scheduled. In the example above, you'd double-click right on 10:30 a.m., and that event would be added at the right time, so when that day arrives, and you're looking at your calendar, you can see that you need to call Lisa in the Accounting department at 10:30 a.m.

X MacTip: Editing or Deleting an Existing Event

Anytime you need to change an existing event, just go to that event and double-click on it to bring up the mini-editor, and then click the Edit button to get the full Event Editor and edit anything about that event (its name, date, time, etc.). If you need to remove an event from your calendar altogether, just click on it and press the Delete key on your keyboard.

Moving an Event to a Different Time or Day

If you need to move an event (we'll use the previous example) to later in the day, in Day or Week view, you can just literally drag-and-drop it to the new time you want (the time listed in your event will update automatically to the new time); however, the Month view just shows the event occurs on that day (because of the size limitations of showing an entire month at once), and you wouldn't know the exact time it's scheduled for without double-clicking on the event. So, that's how you move an event to a different time on the same day, but what if you want the event to move to a different day, or even month? Well, if it's moving to a day in the same week, in Week view, click-and-drag it to the new day and time that week (as shown here, where I dragged my call event from Wednesday at 10:30 a.m. to Friday at 4:00 p.m. Of course, you could press Command-E to bring up the Event Editor and type in Friday's date and time manually, but that's just too much trouble). If you need to move to a different week, just switch to the Month view, and drag-and-drop it on the date you need it. If you do need to move months (or years), that's the one time you will need to press Command-E to bring up the Event Editor and do it there.

Adding a Reminder Alarm to Your Event

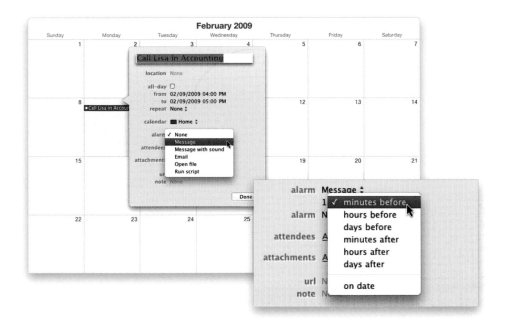

If you need to be reminded about an event (let's just say you can't miss that call with Lisa), then you can set an alarm to go off right at 4:00 p.m. on Friday, or a certain amount of time before, so you're ready for the call. You also get to choose which kind of alarm you want—do you just want a message to pop up onscreen, or do you want that message to also sound an audible alarm? You can even have iCal send you an email reminder— it's up to you. You set these alarms by pressing Command-E to bring up the Event Editor, where you'll see an Alarm pop-up menu with the choices you see in the Event Editor above. When you add an alarm, a little set of options appears below it so you can choose when that alarm should go off (see the close-up above right for an example). Also, when you add an alarm, another Alarm field appears (so, you could set one alarm to send you a message with a sound, and another alarm to email you, and so on), because you can have as many alarms as you'd like (I stopped when I got to adding 11 alarms, which according to my wife is about two short of what I need to remember anything).

X MacTip: Shortcuts for Switching Views

You can switch between Day, Week, and Month view by pressing Command-1 (for Day), Command-2 (for Week), and Command-3 (for Month).

Creating Multiple Color–Coded Calendars

At the beginning of this chapter, I talked about how useful having multiple color-coded calendars can be—now you're going to find out why. By default, iCal comes with two calendars: Home (events appear in blue) and Work (events appear in green). When you want to assign an event to either Home or Work, in the sidebar on the left, click on the calendar you want first, then when you add an event, it's color-coded and tagged to that calendar. If you forgot to click on a calendar first, don't sweat it—you can change which calendar an event is assigned to in the Event Editor, using the Calendar pop-up menu. To create a new color-coded calendar, just click the + (plus sign) button at the bottom left of the window, and it adds a new color-coded calendar (iCal chooses the color for you, but you can change it later—see the tip below), and you can name this new calendar whatever you'd like, then show or hide your different calendars by turning on/off the checkbox beside them in the sidebar on the left.

X MacTip: Changing the Color of Your Calendar

To change the color of a calendar, just Control-click (or Right-click) directly on a calendar (in the sidebar on the left) and choose Get Info. A dialog will pop down from the top of the window, and on the far-right side is a pop-up menu where you can choose a different color or create your own custom color.

Creating Events That Span Hours or Days

If you have a meeting you need to schedule, and you know it's going to span several hours, you can have iCal visually block out that time, and it also works for events that span several days (like your vacation). Here's how to do it in Day view: first, switch to Day view, then click-and-drag out a new event at the time that your meeting will start, and keep dragging downward until the event is scheduled to end. So, let's say your meeting is scheduled to start at 10:00 a.m. and last 4½ hours. Click your cursor right on 10:00 a.m. and drag downward until you reach 2:30 p.m. You can also do this manually in the Event Editor (press Command-E) by increasing the To time field by 4½ hours (as shown above). It works pretty much the same way when you need to span multiple days, but you have to use the Event Editor, because Day view won't let you drag over multiple days, so press Command-E and do it there. When you change the To field to make it days ahead, your event spreads out to cover all those days (but it's a thin bar in Month view, rather than the thick one you see above, because of the compressed size of the monthly calendar). When you're done, just click the Done button and your event now spans from the From to the To block of time.

Repeating an Event

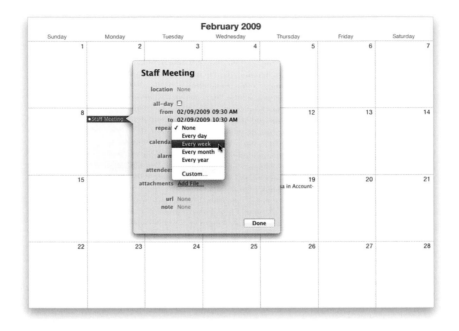

If you have something you need to do every week or every month (like a meeting every Monday at 9:30 a.m. or a bill you need to send out every month), you can schedule any event as a repeating event. Here's how: First create your event on the day and time you need it (for our example, we'll do that 9:30 a.m. Monday meeting). Then press Command-E to bring up the Event Editor. Right below the To field, there's a Repeat pop-up menu where you can choose how often this meeting repeats, as shown above (in our example, this meeting is every Monday, so when you choose Every Week, it adds that event to every Monday from here on out). If you need to schedule something different (like a meeting that happens every two weeks, or every 10 days, etc.), then choose Custom to make that choice. If you need to remove a repeating event on a particular day, just click on it, press Delete, and a dialog will appear asking if you want to remove just that one instance, or all the future events, as well.

Adding a To Do to iCal's To-Do List

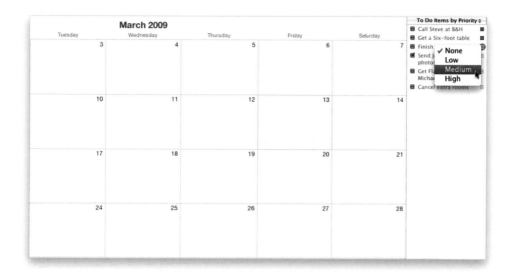

iCal has a built-in To-Do list, and it's a pretty handy place to have a to-do list, since a lot of the things that wind up on your calendar will create things for you to do. To see your To-Do list, click on the little pushpin icon in the bottom-right corner of the iCal window, and it appears on the right side. To add a to-do item to the To-Do list, just double-click on any blank space, and it adds a new item, and it's highlighted so you can type in what you're supposed to do. Once your to-do item has been added to the list, you can assign a priority level to it (High, Medium, or Low) by clicking on the three-bars button to the far right of it. A pop-up menu (shown above) will appear so you can choose the priority for that to do. You can then sort your to dos by their priority (or by a number of other different methods) by clicking on the column header at the top of the To-Do list). You can also just arrange them manually by dragging-and-dropping them into the order you want them.

Editing Your To-Do Items

Once you have a to-do item on your To-Do list, you've got lots of options for what you can do with it. The first is nothing—just leave it right where it is, and when you complete that task, you can turn on the Completed checkbox beside it. If this to-do item needs to be done by a certain date, then double-click on the to-do item itself, and a window similar to the Event Editor pops up (shown above), where you can assign that to-do item to a specific date, so the date will appear above the to do. You can even assign an alarm (see page 75) to remind you to do your to do. When you're done assigning options to your to do, click the Done button. *Note:* To dos you add here in iCal are also added to your To-Do list in Mail, since it's the other most likely place that you'll be when you need to add things to your list (the two are basically synced).

X MacTip: Subscribing to Public Calendars

There are lots of free public iCal calendars you can subscribe to that add dates to your calendar. For example, I subscribe to a calendar that adds each year's Tampa Bay Buccaneers NFL season schedule to my iCal. To find some of these calendars you can subscribe to for free, visit Apple's iCal site at www.apple.com/downloads/macosx/calendars/ or visit iCalShare.com, which has over 2,500 calendars you can subscribe to, with everything from NASA launch dates, to hockey schedules, to movie release dates, to Disney Annual Pass blackout dates. It's amazing to just stop by and see what's available.

Sharing Your Calendar with Other iCal Users

If you'd like to share one (or more) of your calendars with a family member or co-worker (maybe your assistant?), you can publish your calendar to the Web (using either a .Mac account, or a regular Web server), and people you invite can subscribe to your calendar. That way, when you make a change to your calendar (like adding a new event), it automatically updates their calendar with your new event. Here's how it's done: First, in the left sidebar, click on the calendar you want to publish, then go under the Calendar menu (up top) and choose Publish. This brings up the Publish Calendar dialog (shown above) where you get to choose a name for your published calendar, how it gets published (on .Mac, if you're a member, or your Web server, in which case it will ask for your server address, username, and password), and how much of your calendar you want published (just the events, or also to dos, or alarms, etc.). Once you've made your choices, click the Publish button and it puts your calendar up online, and gives you the address where it's found (and a button to email that link to the people you choose). For those people to subscribe to your calendar, all they have to do is launch their iCal, then go under the Calendar menu and choose Subscribe. When the Subscribe to Calendar dialog appears, have them enter the Web address where your calendar was published and hit the Subscribe button, and they're subscribed—that's it. If they turn on the Auto-Refresh option (in the subsequent dialog), they can choose to have iCal check daily (or hourly) to see if you've updated your calendar, and then it updates theirs.

More Address Book Tips

X MacTip: Making Phone Numbers Easier to Read

Just Control-click (or Right-click) on the number and choose Large Type. This will display the number on your screen really, really, really big. Like crazy mondo big. (Try it—you'll see.)

X MacTip: Sending Email to a Group

If you created a group, and you want to send an email to everyone in that group at once, just Control-click (or Right-click) on the group, and then choose Send Email to "Group Name" from the contextual menu. This brings up a new email message window already addressed to everyone in that group. All you have to do is type in your message and hit Send.

X MacTip: Instant Directions to Your Contact's Address

Want to get directions to a contact's house or business? Just Control-click (or Right-click) on their address in Address Book, and choose Map Of from the contextual menu. This brings up their location in Google Maps, and you can choose Get Directions to Here on the map.

X MacTip: Quick Spotlight Search of a Contact

If you find someone in your Address Book and you want to do a quick search of your entire Mac for their name, just Control-click (or Right-click) on their name in the Address Book's Name column, and choose Spotlight: "Name."

X MacTip: Merge Two Similar Contacts Together

If you have two Address Book contacts that are similar, you can merge them into one contact by selecting both of them, then pressing Command-| (it's with the backslash on your keyboard) to merge them together.

More iCal Tips

X MacTip: Adding iCal Events from Within Mail

If someone emails you a message, and that message has a date in it (maybe an appointment, or meeting, or party, etc.), just move your cursor over the date, and a little down-facing arrow will appear to its right, letting you know that you can Control-click (or Right-click) on that date and a contextual menu will appear where you can choose Create New iCal Event, and it will take you to that day in your calendar and create a new blank event—all you have to do is start typing.

X MacTip: Quickly Change the Order of Your Calendars in the Sidebar

Just click, hold, and drag them into the order you'd like.

X MacTip: Assign Calendars by Dragging-and-Dropping

If you've created a new event, and you want to change the calendar it's assigned to, just drag-and-drop the event right onto the calendar you want it to be in, in the sidebar.

X MacTip: Creating Groups of Calendars

If you have a number of calendars that are related (for example, you have calendars for different divisions of your company), you can organize things by grouping them together. Just Shift-click on the Add a New Calendar button (it's the + [plus sign] in the bottom-left corner), and it creates a Group that you can drag-and-drop other calendars into or create new calendars under.

X MacTip: Put Live Links into Your New Events

If your new event is a reminder to visit a website, just add angle brackets around the Web address—like this: <http://www.apple.com>—and you can click on the link to jump to that page.

Chapter Four

Unlocking Your Mac's Dashboard

How to Make Your Mac Bring You the Info You Need

 We spend a lot of our time looking for stuff—news, sports scores, the weather, stock quotes, clothes to buy online, we monitor eBay auctions, and do a lot of research on everyday things every day. Now, what if your Mac could do the searching for you, and when you woke up in the morning you would go to your Mac, press one button, and it would bring all that information—stuff that you yourself chose—right to you? You wouldn't have to go to a single website—all your stock quotes, weather for your town, your flight status for that day, news, eBay auctions, and any one of the hundreds of things you choose could be right there waiting for you each morning. Wouldn't that be cool? It sure would be. Now if only your Mac had a feature like that. Unfortunately, it doesn't, so you'd better set your alarm an hour or so earlier so you can get up and start gathering all this information, because you don't want to start your day without it. Now, although your Mac doesn't have that feature, mine actually does. That's right, you see I have high-level connections deep within Apple itself, so they customize special "secret" versions of Mac OS X Leopard just for me with features I alone can access. For example, they added a special feature to my Mac called "Dashboard," where all this information is brought to me by just clicking on a Dashboard icon down in the Dock (don't bother looking down in your Dock, it's not there, because this is a feature strictly for cool insiders like me, with levels of access others can only dream about). I'm sure you understand they can't give out features like Dashboard to just anyone, or then everyone would have that kind of power right at their fingertips. That's not to say that one day in the distant future you won't look down in your Dock and see something like Dashboard, but when you do, just know that I've already moved on to something even more secretive and special called "Time Machine", which, of course, is only on my Mac and my Mac alone.

Launching Dashboard

Dashboard is one of my all-time favorite Mac OS features, because if you take just a few minutes and set it up now, it can save literally hours each week. Here's why: most people spend a certain amount of time each day (or numerous times a day), digging up things like the weather, what their stocks are doing, looking up things in the dictionary, digging up phone numbers, checking to see what's playing at the movie theater, etc., and this takes us hopping from website to website to website to gather all this info. But what if all this info was already waiting for you? What if you only went to one place, and it was already gathered for you? That's what Dashboard does—it gathers the info you want and brings it to you, instead of you going and tracking it down all over the Web. To launch Dashboard, you can either click on the Dashboard icon down in the Dock (as shown here), or simply press F4 on your key-board (F12 on older keyboards). The Dashboard "widgets" (that's Apple's name for those little applications that do all your bidding) appear right over whatever you were last working on, but they are easy to see, because when you open Dashboard, it dims the screen behind your widgets.

Using the Built-In Widgets (i.e., Weather)

Leopard comes with a number of widgets, and there are literally thousands more you can download for free, but for now let's learn how one of those built-in widgets works, because once you get the hang of one, they all kinda work similarly. So first, make Dashboard visible (click on its Dock icon or press F4 on your keyboard or F12 on older keyboards). One of the most popular is the Weather widget (shown above). By default, it shows you the weather in Cupertino, California (where Apple is headquartered), but you can change it to almost any city you'd like by moving your cursor over the widget. When you do this, a tiny "i" button will appear in the bottom-right corner of the widget. Click on that tiny "i" and this flips the widget over to reveal its control panel, where you can either enter a city, state, or zip code in the search field. Now press the Return key on your keyboard, and as long as you're connected to the Internet, it will search for your city. When it finds your city (it just takes seconds), it will display it in the search field. If it doesn't find your city (perhaps you live in a really small city—pop. 241), you can choose a nearby larger city, which it's more likely to find. There's also a checkbox that lets you display the low temperature for the city you're going to be monitoring. When you click the Done button, it turns back around and displays the current weather conditions and forecast for that city (it actually goes to Accuweather.com to gather the latest weather report), and will update each day automatically when you open Dashboard.

Adding More Widgets
(Monitoring More Cities)

So now you're monitoring one city, but what if you want to add another (maybe an international city, like Milan, Italy)? Luckily, you can monitor as many cities as you have space left on your screen (you can transform your computer into one big weather monitoring station, if you like). To monitor more cities, press F4 on your keyboard (F12 on older keyboards) and click the Open (+) button that appears in the bottom-left corner of your screen. This brings up the Widget Bar, with all the widgets that come with Mac OS X Leopard (and it's also where you'll access any free widgets you download from the Web). They're displayed in alphabetical order, and the widget you want is called Weather, so you're going to have to scroll over to the right to reach the Ws. You'll see a little arrow on the far right, and each time you click it, it scrolls you over to the next set of widgets, so go ahead and click this arrow once or twice until you see the Weather widget appear. Now just click once on it, and it will appear onscreen, with a little ripple effect around it so you see right where it was added. You'll configure this Weather widget just like you did the previous one (by clicking on the little "i" button). You can add as many of this Weather widget as you'd like—just keep clicking on that Weather widget in the Widget Bar, and it'll keep adding them. By the way, if you prefer, rather than just clicking, you can drag-and-drop widgets from the Widget Bar right out onto your desktop. It doesn't change anything; it's just more fun. When you're done adding widgets, press the Close (X) button (where the Open button used to be in the bottom-left corner) to hide the Widget Bar.

Closing Widgets

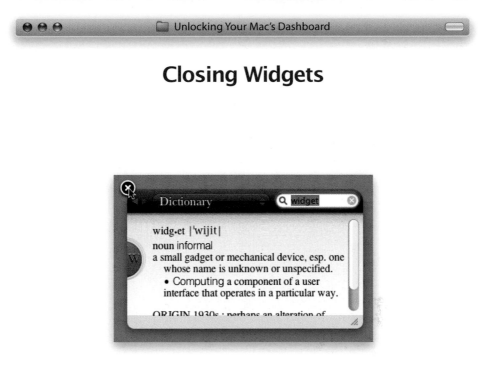

If you decide your want to close a widget (this just removes it from your Dashboard view—it doesn't remove the widget from your computer), first press-and-hold the Option key on your keyboard, then move your cursor over the widget you want to close, and a small round button with an X inside it will appear just outside the top-left corner of the widget. Click on that X to close the widget. To bring that widget back again, click the Open (+) button in the bottom left of your screen to bring back the Widget Bar, then click on the icon for the widget you closed.

Hiding Widgets You Don't Need

If you start downloading a lot of widgets (hey, it's easy to get hooked on these things), and your Widget Bar starts getting really long, you can choose which widgets stay visible in your Widget Bar and which ones are hidden from view. You do this by bringing up Dashboard (F4 on your keyboard or F12 on older keyboards), then clicking the Open (+) button in the bottom-left corner, and then clicking on the Manage Widgets button that appears to the right of the Close button (see above). This brings up the Manage Widgets dialog, which is simple to use. Just turn off the checkbox beside any widget you want hidden, then close the dialog by clicking on the little X button in the upper-left corner. Now, only the widgets that you left turned on will appear in your Widget Bar, which shortens your scrolling, and cuts down the clutter big time. If you ever want those widgets back, just go back to the Manage Widgets dialog and turn their checkboxes back on.

Getting More Widgets

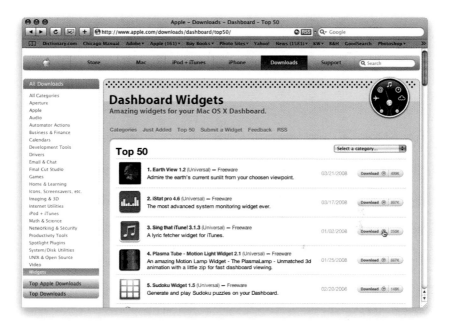

Half the fun of using widgets is finding and downloading widgets to gather even more info for you, and they have everything from widgets that can track your flights, to widgets that bring you song lyrics for songs on your iPod, to widgets that are simply games. To find more widgets, open Dashboard (F4 on your keyboard or F12 on older keyboards), then click the Open (+) button in the lower-left corner to open the Widget Bar. Once it appears, click the Manage Widgets button, and in the Manage Widgets dialog that appears, click the More Widgets button. This takes you to Apple's main Dashboard webpage, which gives you access to a library of literally thousands of free downloadable widgets. You can look at a listing of the top widgets or search by category, and when you see one you like, you just download it and it installs for you automatically. Then, to access your newly downloaded widgets, you simply choose them from your Widget Bar.

Deleting Widgets

If you want to permanently delete a widget (maybe it's one you downloaded, and you decided you don't like it, or won't use it), you can delete one by opening Dashboard (F4 on your keyboard or F12 on older keyboards), then clicking the Open (+) button at the bottom left of the screen to bring up the Widget Bar. Now, click the Manage Widgets button to the immediate right of the Close button to bring up the Manage Widgets dialog. To delete a widget you've downloaded (you can only delete widgets you've downloaded—the default widgets that come with Mac OS X Leopard can't be deleted), you just click on the round, red button with a minus sign (–) that appears to the right of the widget's name. This brings up a warning dialog that asks if you want to Move This Widget to the Trash. If that's what you want to do, click the OK button and it moves it to the Trash for you. Now close the Manage Widgets dialog and the Widgets Bar, and that puppy is gone!

Other Ways to Bring Up Dashboard

Besides clicking on the Dock icon or pressing F4 on your keyboard (F12 on older keyboards), there are a number of other ways you can bring up Dashboard. You choose these by going under the Apple menu and choosing System Preferences. When the System Preferences dialog appears, click on Exposé & Spaces. When that preference pane appears, click on the Exposé tab, and at the bottom of this pane there is a pop-up menu that lets you choose a different F-key for opening Dashboard (so if you wanted to use F4 for something else, you can choose to have Dashboard open with a different F-key—just select it from the Hide and Show pop-up menu). However, you can also have Dashboard open when you move your cursor to a specific corner of the screen (for example, you could have it open when you move your cursor to the bottom-left corner of the screen). You choose this option at the top of this Exposé pane. In the Active Screen Corners section at the top, in the pop-up menu closest to the bottom-left corner of the screen thumbnail, choose Dashboard (as shown above), then close the Preferences dialog. Now when you move your cursor down into that corner of the screen, Dashboard will open.

X **MacTip: Bring Up Dashboard by Right-Clicking**

If you have a two-button mouse, you can go to your System Preferences, click on Keyboard & Mouse, then click on the Mouse tab, and from the pop-up menu for the right button, choose to have it bring up Dashboard. Then you're just one click away.

Creating Web Clips

One of the coolest widgets introduced in Mac OS X Leopard was the Web Clips widget, which kind of lets you create your own custom widget from any webpage. Here's how it works: let's say there's a webpage that you like to get information from (let's say it's a bestseller list for your industry), you can bring up the Web Clips widget, capture just that part of the webpage as a Web clip, and that part of the page will now appear as a widget on your Dashboard. The cool thing is, as that part of the webpage gets updated each day, it automatically updates your Web clip widget, as well. That way, each day you'll get that list, without having to go to that webpage. Here's how to create your own Web Clip widget: Launch the Safari Web browser, then go to the webpage that has an area you want as a Web clip. Click the Web Clip button up in Safari's toolbar (it's the one with the scissors icon), then click-and-drag your cursor over the area on this webpage you want saved as a Web clip and press the Return key (which is the shortcut for the Add button). That's it—you've created a Web clip that will update automatically anytime the content in that area you selected gets updated. Pretty slick—I know.

My Favorite Widgets

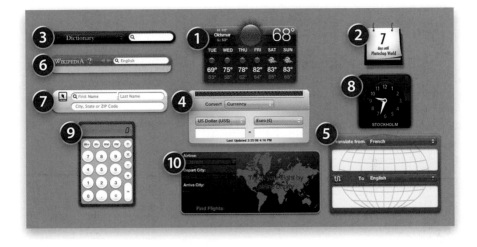

Here are 10 of my favorite widgets, and what they do:

1) **Weather**—I monitor the next three cities I'm traveling to.

2) **Countdown**—I keep an eye on how long it is before any major event, like Photoshop World, or Macworld Expo, or my vacation.

3) **Dictionary/Thesaurus**—I use this daily when writing books and articles. Indispensable.

4) **Unit Converter**—I use the currency converter when buying things from other countries.

5) **Translation**—I get emails from readers of my books from around the world. This helps.

6) **Wikipedia**—This saves me a trip to the Web (especially good for pop culture and learning about people in my industry).

7) **White Pages**—Again, it just saves me from searching around the Web.

8) **World Clock**—Anytime a friend is traveling, or I'm traveling, or I'm working with someone in another time zone, I have a clock open for that time zone.

9) **Calculator**—It keeps me from having one in my Dock.

10) **Flight Tracker**—Clearly, I travel too much.

More Tips for Using Dashboard

X MacTip: See All the Weather Widget's Weather Icons

If you want to see all the possible weather icons that the Weather widget can display, just press-and-hold Command-Option and click on the icon at the top center of the widget (the sun, the clouds, the moon, the snow, etc.). Each time you click, it shows another one of the icons for a town called Nowhere.

X MacTip: Getting More Detailed Weather Info

If you click directly to the left of the city's name in the Weather widget, it opens your Web browser and takes you to the full Accuweather.com page for that city, with detailed information about that city's weather.

X MacTip: How to Monitor Weather in More Than One City

You can keep clicking-and-dragging as many Weather widgets as you'd like right out onto your desktop, and then click the little "i" icon on the new widgets to choose the cities you want to monitor.

X MacTip: From Your Yellow Pages Widget to Your Address Book

If you look up a company in the Business (Yellow Pages) widget, you can add that company's address and phone number to your Mac's Address Book by clicking on the little + (plus sign) that appears to the left of the address.

X MacTip: Getting "The Big Number" Using the Address Book Widget

If you're using Dashboard's Address Book widget, and you'd like to see your contact's phone number larger, just click on a contact's phone number and it displays in really large numbers right across your screen.

More Tips for Using Dashboard

MacTip: Putting Widgets Where You Want Them from the Start

If you open the Widget Bar and just click on a widget to add it to Dashboard, by default, it appears centered onscreen, and then you can click-and-drag it where you want it. If you'd rather it just appear right where you want it from the beginning, don't click on it, instead, drag-and-drop it right out of the Widget Bar to right where you want it onscreen.

MacTip: Moving Widgets Where You Want Them

You can organize your widgets onscreen any way you'd like them—just click-and-drag them right where you want them.

MacTip: Shortcut for Finding More Widgets

If you want to add more widgets to your Dashboard, just Control-click (Right-click) on the Dashboard icon down in the Dock, and a contextual menu will appear, where you can choose More Widgets and this takes you directly to Apple's Dashboard Widgets webpage, where you can download literally thousands of free widgets.

MacTip: Which Widgets Are Editable

Many widgets, like the Weather widget, let you edit or customize how the widget works, but some widgets are "one-trick ponies" (they do one specific thing, so you can't edit or change the way they operate—they do one thing and that's it). So, how do you know if you can edit a widget? Just move your cursor over the widget and if you can customize or edit it, a little "i" icon will appear in the bottom-right corner of the widget. If the "i" icon doesn't appear, you can't edit that widget.

Chapter Five

Getting Email on Your Mac

Plus, How to Leverage Your Mac's Mail to Keep Organized

When it comes to naming products and features, I think Apple has pretty much cornered the market on cool names. For example, how about "Time Machine" for something that lets you retrieve files you deleted weeks or months ago? Or how about "AirPort" (for wireless connections), and then of course there's the iPod, and iTunes, and well…you get the picture. But perhaps the simplest of all names is what Apple calls your Mac's email program—it's simply, "Mail." Even the icon is iconic—a postage stamp. I'm actually glad they didn't name it "Email," or then I'd have a lot of confusing sounding sentences, like "To send an email, launch Email, and inside Email, click the New Email button." I think perhaps the most amazing thing about the name "Mail" is that no other software program had used it yet. Everyone was coming up with all these clever-sounding names, yet no one had taken the cleverest name of all. This got me thinking, "How many other ingeniously simple and incredibly descriptive product names are just sitting out there, waiting for someone to strike gold?" For example, if I were to come up with a line of sneakers, I would call it "Sneakers." Then every time parents would tell their kids, "It's time to go to school—go get your sneakers on," it would be a mini-promo for my product. When you start thinking about this, it makes your mind reel. Creating new sandwich bread? Call it "Bread." Goodyear introduces a new tire; it should be called "Tire." Think of how easy this would make our lives—you'd never have to utter the phrase, "What was that thing called, again?" because the name would also be the description. That's precisely why I named this book exactly what it is—*The Mac OS X Leopard Book* (I actually wanted to shorten it to just "Book," but I couldn't get my publisher to go for it).

Setting Up Your Email Account

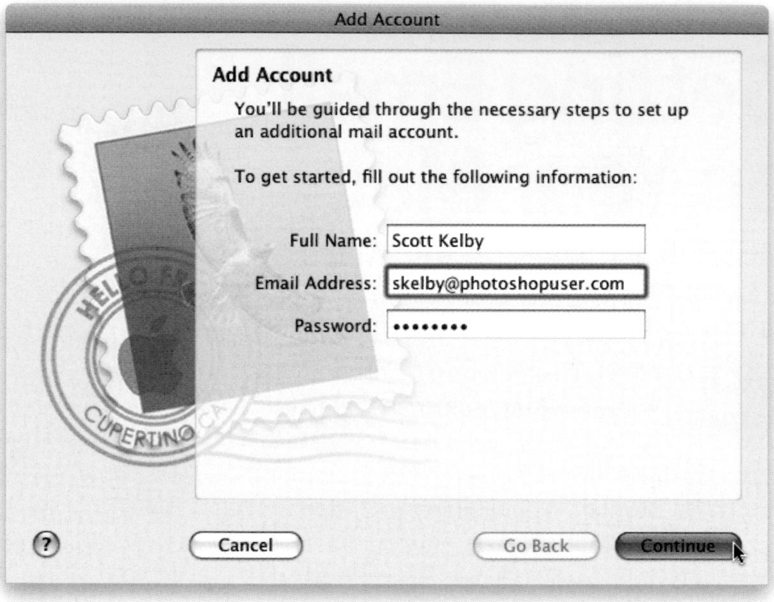

Add Account

Add Account

You'll be guided through the necessary steps to set up
an additional mail account.

To get started, fill out the following information:

Full Name: Scott Kelby

Email Address: skelby@photoshopuser.com

Password: ••••••••

(?)   (Cancel)   (Go Back)   **Continue**

I encourage all my friends to use Apple's own email program (called simply, "Mail")
because: (1) it's so easy to set up and use, (2) it's surprisingly powerful and has some
very clever features, and (3) it ties directly into your Mac's other applications in a way
that will absolutely make your life easier. Start by launching the Mail application
(it's in the Dock, and its icon looks like a postage stamp). When you launch Mail, it
brings up a "Welcome to Mail" dialog. You don't have to do anything here, just click
the Continue button, but before you do that, you'll need to get some info from your
ISP (Internet Service Provider) that you're going to be asked in the following screens,
so have this info in front of you first. You're going to need to know: (1) whether you have
a POP email account or an IMAP account (your service provider can tell you all this stuff);
(2) you'll need your email username and password; (3) you'll need your current email
address (like yourname@tampabay.rr.com); and (4) you'll need the name of your
incoming and outgoing mail server (again, all this comes from the company that
provides your email service). Now you can click that Continue button, and the screen
above appears. Enter your name (just the regular name your mom gave you), your
email address, and your email password, then click the Continue button.

Setting Things Up to Receive Incoming Mail

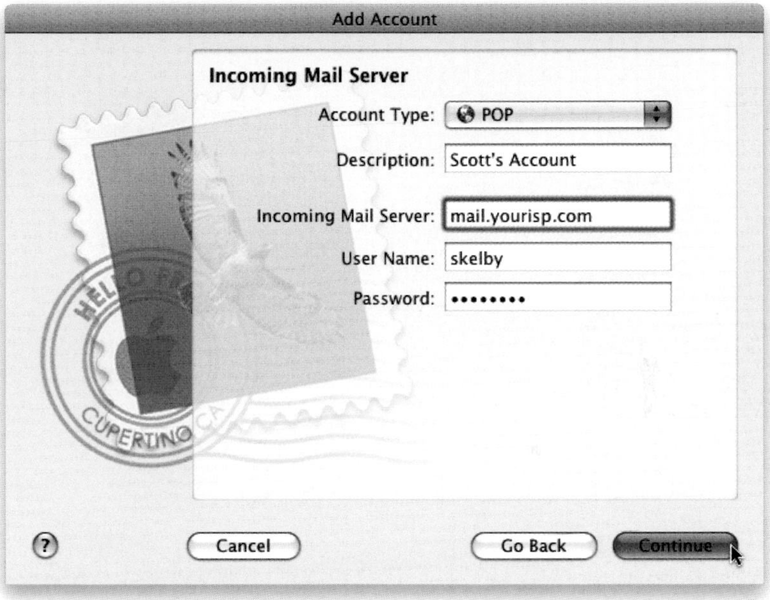

Once you click Continue, it brings up the screen shown above, where you type in the Incoming Mail Server info that you got from your ISP. At the top, choose the Account Type (POP, IMAP, or Exchange. If you have a .Mac account membership with Apple, choose .Mac). Because you might wind up having more than one email account, give this account a descriptive name (like "Scott's Account," or "Scott's Yahoo email," but use your own name, instead. Sorry, I couldn't help myself). The next field down is where you enter your Incoming Mail Server info, and it's usually something like what you see above (mail.yourisp.com), then enter your email username (this is actually what appears before the @ in your email address) and password, and click the Continue button. When you click Continue, it goes to that server and checks to make sure the server information you entered here is correct.

Setting Things Up So You Can Send Email

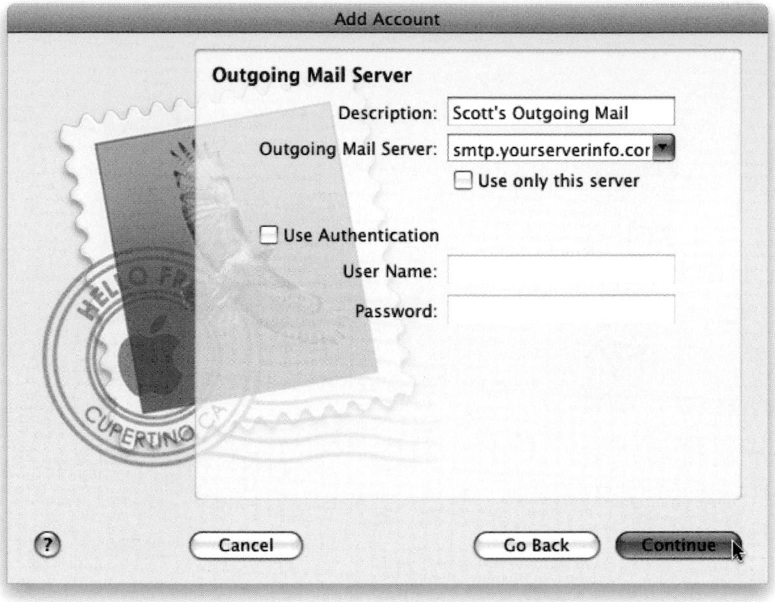

To be able to send email, you'll have to enter some info in this next screen, too. At the top, enter your description (this is just for you), and your outgoing mail server (it's usually something like smtp.yourserverinfo.com). You can skip the whole Use Authentication thing, and just move on by clicking the Continue button, and you'll be taken to the Outgoing Mail Security screen. You can also skip this screen, so just click the Continue button to go to the final screen (you're almost there).

One Final Step and You're Done

This last screen just confirms all the information you've entered (this is kind of like the summary screen you see when you're about to buy something from an online store). If everything looks right, click the Create button, and it creates this new account. You'll see it now in the top-left side of the Mail window, within Mailboxes, under Inbox. That's it—you're ready to get and send mail.

Sending an Email Message

To send an email message, just click on the New Message button in the top middle of the Mail window, and it brings up a New Message window (seen above). In the To field, enter the address of the person you're sending it to. If you'd like a copy of the email sent to someone else at the same time, enter their address in the Cc field. (*Note*: When you copy someone on an email, the person you send the original email to will be able to see that you copied this email to someone else, and they'll also see that person's email address, as well. Just so you know.) Then, in the big blank window below all that, start writing your email. When you're done, press the Send button in the upper-left corner of the New Message window and off it goes! By the way, if you want to email more than one person, just type in their addresses, separated by a comma, right after the first address up in the To field.

X MacTip: Sending a Copy of Your Email Privately

If you want to send someone a private copy of an email (so the original person you're sending the email to won't know that you sent a copy to someone else), go under Mail's View menu and choose Bcc Address Field (Bcc stands for "blind carbon copy"). This adds a new Bcc address field under the Cc (carbon copy) field, and when you enter an email address in this field, a copy of the email is sent to that address, but the fact you sent a copy is hidden from the original person you emailed.

Customizing Your Email Text

Mail lets you customize your email by adding color to your text, changing fonts and font size, adding bold and italic, and even adding pre-designed templates with graphics. To change the color of some text, just highlight it, then click on the Colors button in the toolbar at the top of the window to bring up the Colors panel you see above. Now, there's kind of a weird thing about the Colors panel: when you bring up the panel, it looks like you've already chosen a color, but your text still looks black. That's because you have to move that little white dot in the color wheel. You can move it just a little, and then move it right back—but once you do move it, you'll see your highlighted text update with your new color. By the way, here's how the Colors panel works: you choose the color you want using the round color wheel, and you choose how dark (or light) that color is using the slider on the right side of the panel. When that slider is up at the top, the color wheel shows the brightest colors. As you click-and-drag the slider down, the colors in the wheel get darker. For white, click-and-drag the little white dot to the center. To get black, click-and-drag the slider all the way to the bottom. You change fonts in a similar way—just highlight the text you want to change, then click on the Fonts button up in the toolbar. When the Fonts panel appears, just choose the font you want from the Family column and it changes right on the spot. If that font has a bold or italic version, you can choose that from the Typeface column. The last column lets you choose your font size. When you're done "fonting," just close the Fonts panel by clicking on the red Close button in the top-left corner of the panel (it's the first button on the left, and it will turn red when you move your cursor over it).

Using Email Templates

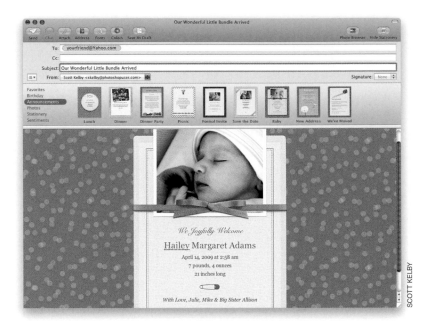

SCOTT KELBY

Mail comes with a number of professionally designed email templates (Apple calls these "stationery"), which you can customize with your own photos and text (as shown above, where I changed the photo and the text). To access these templates, click on the New Message button, then in the New Message window, click on the Show Stationery button in the top-right corner, and your stationery choices will appear right above the body of your email. There are a number of categories to choose from (along the left side), so you would choose your category first, then click on the template you'd like, and it's added as your email message. If the template has a photo, it's just a placeholder, and you can put your own photo in its place by clicking on the Photo Browser button in the top right of the window, which opens the Photo Browser and lets you access your iPhoto library of photos. Find a photo you want, and then just drag-and-drop it onto the placeholder photo. To customize the text, just click once on the placeholder text and type in your custom text.

Setting Up Your Email Signature

If you use your Mac for business, you may want to have the option of having Mail automatically add your full name, company, title, and contact info at the bottom of your email message (actually, you can have it add anything you'd like there, like a favorite quotation, or "Go Bucs!" if you're a Tampa Bay Buccaneers fan like me, but I used the contact info example because it's so common). These are called "signatures" and you can create multiple signatures so you can have one for work, one for friends, one for people you really don't want to give all your contact info to, and so on. To create a signature, go under the Mail menu (up in the menu bar at the top of the screen), and choose Preferences. When the Preferences dialog appears, click on the Signatures icon, and when those preferences appear, in the first column click on the email account that you want to have access to the signatures you're about to create. Next, click the + (plus sign) button at the bottom of the center column and a new signature is added to that center column—it's highlighted so you can give it a name. Then, in the third column, type in the text you'd like to appear as your signature (your name and email address have already been added for you). When you're done, close the Preferences dialog by clicking on the red Close button in the upper-left corner. Now when you're writing an email, by default, Mail will add the first signature you entered. To change your signature, just choose the one you want from the Signature pop-up menu found at the top right of the message window, under the Subject field. To start with a blank email each time and only add the signature if you want it, go back to Mail's Signatures preferences, click on the account you want to change the default for, then choose None from the Choose Signature pop-up menu at the bottom.

Checking for Incoming Email

Anytime you launch Mail, it automatically checks for incoming mail, and then it checks every five minutes after that (as long as you have Mail open, that is). If you want it to check either more frequently or less f requently, go under the Mail menu and choose Preferences, then click on the General icon up top. From the Check for New Mail pop-up menu, you can choose to have it check from every minute to up to once an hour (and a few other times in between)—it's totally up to you (but the Every 5 Minutes default choice is actually pretty good, and it's the one I use). If you're expecting an important email now, and don't want to wait until five minutes go by, just click the Get Mail button in the top left of the Mail window, and it will check for email for all your email accounts right now. If you have more than one email account, but only want to check mail for one particular account, don't click the Get Mail button. Instead, go under the Mailbox menu, under Get New Mail, and then choose the individual email account you want it to check, and the others will remain unchecked (well, at least until five minutes goes by).

Replying to Email

If someone sends you an email and you want to reply back to it, just click the Reply button in the toolbar at the top of the Mail window. It opens a new message window, already addressed to the person who sent you the email, and it even includes the original message they sent you, but their message appears in blue, so it's easy to see which is the old message (in blue) and which is the new reply message (in black). If a number of people have been included or copied on this email, you can have your reply emailed to them all by clicking the Reply All button in the toolbar, instead.

⊠ MacTip: Just Quoting One Part of Their Email Message

By default, when you hit the Reply button, it displays the entire original email message you were sent. If you only want to address one or two sentences in the email, just highlight those sentences before you hit the Reply button, and then only those highlighted sentences will appear in your reply.

Sending a Photo or File with Your Email

There are a number of different ways to send someone a photo, including sending the photo from right within iPhoto (see Chapter 8), but if you're already in Mail, there's a quicker way: just create a new email message, then click on the Photo Browser button up in the top-right corner of the message window to give you access to all your photos in iPhoto and Photo Booth. When you find the photo you want to send, just drag-and-drop it into the body of your email message. If the photo you want to send isn't in iPhoto, then you'll love this shortcut: just drag-and-drop the photo file right onto the Mail icon in the Dock. This will launch Mail and automatically attach your photo to a new blank email message (as shown above)—all you have to do is address it. This also works with any type of file you want to attach (Excel spreadsheets, Word documents, PDF files—you name it), just drag-and-drop the file onto the Mail icon in the Dock. There's another method, but it's a bit more manual, so I don't use it often: once you've opened a new email message window, you can click on the Attach button in the toolbar, and it will bring up the standard Mac Open dialog, and you can navigate to the file you want to include and click Choose File. All these methods work (the last one just takes too many steps for me).

Organizing Your Email

When email arrives in your Inbox, it's marked as Unread (with a blue dot on its left), so you can quickly see which emails you've read or not (once you click on an email, the email message is displayed, so the blue Unread dot goes away). If you've quickly scanned an email, but didn't have time to read the whole thing, you can mark it as Unread so it gets the blue dot back again, and reminds you to read it when you get more time. To do that, press the keyboard shortcut Command-Shift-U. If you have an email you want to come back to, you can flag it (it literally puts a little orange flag icon to the left of it) to get your attention. To flag an email message, just click on the message, and then from the Message menu, choose Mark and then choose As Flagged (or use the keyboard shortcut Command-Shift-L). If you quickly want to see just your flagged emails, click on the Flag icon at the top-left corner of your column titles in the main email window.

⌧ MacTip: Keeping Important Emails for Future Reference

If you have emails you want to keep for future reference (maybe they're online receipts for things you've purchased, or instructions on how to do something), you can create a folder that lives on the left side of your Mail window and you can drag-and-drop those emails right in there—just click on the + (plus sign) button at the bottom-left side of the window and choose New Mailbox from the pop-up menu. That way, your important "keeper" emails are just one click away.

Dealing with Junk Mail (Spam)

If you're getting your fair share of junk mail from solicitors selling everything from name-brand watches to prescription drugs, you can turn on Mail's built-in Junk Mail filter, which looks for obvious spam emails and puts them in a Junk mailbox (instead of in your Inbox). To turn this filtering on, go under the Mail menu and choose Preferences, then click the Junk Mail icon up top to see the Junk Mail preferences. First, turn on the checkbox for Enable Junk Mail Filtering (if it's not already turned on). Just below that, you get to choose what Mail does with that junk mail when it arrives. I don't even want to see junk mail, so I have it moved to the Junk mailbox (as shown here), but if you're paranoid that Mail might accidentally move an important email to the Junk mailbox, you can have it all pour into your Inbox, and the messages it thinks are junk will have a gold Junk icon beside them to help you quickly see what's what. If you get a message like this (with a gold Junk icon to the left of it) and it's not actually junk, just click on the Not Junk button in the toolbar at the top of the Mail window, which changes the gold Junk icon to the blue Unread dot.

X MacTip: Checking Your Junk Mailbox, Just in Case

I have Mail automatically move all suspected junk mail into the Junk mailbox, so I don't have it cluttering up my Inbox, and if you do this too, I recommend doing what I do: click on the Junk mailbox once a week and take a quick look to see who sent the emails, just in case one slipped by Mail's Junk Mail filter and a real email got marked as Junk. It just takes two minutes once a week, and if you find one that slipped by, it's worth it.

Parental Controls for Email

If your kids have their own email accounts, you can protect them from receiving emails from strangers or solicitors by turning on Mail's built-in Parental Controls. You don't actually do this from within Mail, because it's part of the Mac operating system, so go under the Apple menu and choose System Preferences. Then, click on the Parental Controls icon (it's in the fourth row down, under System). You then have to choose which account you want to apply Parental Controls to (so, you'd click on your child's account), and then click on the Enable Parental Controls button. In the following pane, click the Mail & iChat tab at the top to bring up those preferences (shown above). First, turn on the Limit Mail checkbox at the top and then click the + (plus sign) button in the middle of the window and a dialog pops down where you can enter the name and email address of people your child is allowed to receive email from. If someone emails your child who is not on this list, if you turn on the Send Permission Requests To checkbox at the bottom of the Mail & iChat pane and enter your email address, it will forward their email to you (instead of your child) and you can decide whether to allow or reject the email from being forwarded to your child. When you're done, close the System Preferences window by pressing Command-W (the shortcut for Close window).

Mail's Built-In To-Do List and Notes

Mail has two built-in features to help you stay organized: (1) A To-Do feature, and what's nice about this feature is that it's in a place where people send you stuff to do (your email Inbox), so it's really handy that you don't have to leave Mail to create a to do. To create a new to do, just click on the To Do button in the toolbar at the top of Mail, and it adds a new to do in your main email window and you can just type in your to do right there. Anytime you want to see your To-Do list, click on To Do in the Reminders section, in the left-side column of Mail. (So, to recap: to create a new to do, click the To Do button up top. To see your To-Do list, click on the To Do link in the left side of the window.) When a to do is complete, turn on the checkbox beside it. (2) Besides the To-Do feature, if you just need to take a quick note, click on the Note button in the toolbar (it's right beside the To Do button), and it brings up a little notepad for jotting down a quick note. When you're done writing your note, click the Done button at the top of the notepad and it adds that note to your Inbox, like it was an email, but it's in a different font and has a note icon to the left of it, so you can see it's a note at a quick glance. If you want your note to become a to do, double-click on it, then click on the To Do button, at the top right of the notepad.

⊠ MacTip: Your To Dos Get Added to iCal Automatically

When you create a to do in Mail, those to dos automatically get added to the To-Do list in iCal (your Mac's calendar program; see Chapter 3), so you can access your to dos in either application (which is smart, because these are the two places to dos wind up being created).

Using Mail's RSS Reader

You can use Mail's built-in RSS reader to monitor all the blogs and news sites you normally go to, and when one of those blogs (news sites, etc.) has a new post, it adds just that post, complete with graphics, to a special section in Mail. This makes keeping up with a lot of information very easy (and fast), because you don't have to go to all of these sites one by one to see if they've posted anything new—Mail will check for you, and only bring you the ones that have posted something new. To add an RSS feed to Mail, first go to the website and copy the Web address (highlight the address and press Command-C to Copy it into memory). Then go under Mail's File menu and choose Add RSS Feeds, and a dialog pops down from the top. Click on the Specify a Custom Feed URL radio button and a field will appear (seen above) where you can paste that Web address you copied earlier (click in that field, then press Command-V to Paste the URL). Now click the Add button, and Mail starts keeping track of that blog for you. If a new post comes in for that blog (news site, etc.), you'll see it in the left-side column in Mail under the RSS section, and the number of new posts appears right after its name (if there's no number, there are no new posts for that site). To see the new posts in your Mail window, click on the site's name in your RSS list. That's all there is to it; now go add some blogs (news sites, etc.)!

Doing Text & Audio Chats Using iChat

iChat

Account Setup

Enter your user name and password. iChat supports .Mac, AIM, Google Talk and Jabber accounts.

Or, you can skip this step by pressing continue.

Account Type: AIM Account

Screen Name: Scott

Password: ••••••••

Get an iChat Account...

Go Back   Continue

Your Mac comes with a very cool little application for doing text, audio, and even video chats called iChat, and it takes just a minute to get it up and running and start chatting with your friends, co-workers, and generally kill your overall productivity. Here's how to set it up: When you first launch iChat (its icon looks like a blue cartoon bubble), a welcome window appears. Click the Continue button and then it will ask you to enter your username and password. If you signed up for a .Mac account, then all you have to do is choose .Mac Account from the Account Type pop-up menu, then enter your .Mac member name and password, and click the Continue button. If you're not a .Mac member, then you'll either need to sign up for .Mac (click the Get an iChat Account button), or you can sign up for one of the free online chat services (like AOL's AIM, Google Talk, or Jabber), but you have to do that at their respective websites (see the tip below). Once you sign up for your account, just choose which service you created your account with from the Account Type pop-up menu in iChat, enter your username and password, click the Continue button, and you're done.

X MacTip: Where to Get a Free Instant Messaging Account

To get a free AIM account, go to www.aim.com, then from the AIM.com menu, choose Get a Screen Name. For a free Google Talk account, go to www.google.com/talk. For a free Jabber account, visit www.jabber.org.

Adding the Friends You Want to Chat With

AIM Buddy List

Scott
Available ▾

Enter the buddy's AIM or .Mac account:

Account Name: jeffk   AIM

Add to Group: Buddies

First Name: Jeff

Last Name: Kelby

Cancel   Add

Once you actually click the Continue button, your Buddy List window appears, but at this point, you don't have any buddies, so you have no one to chat with. Now, I'm assuming you have friends with computers, or you wouldn't even be reading how to chat, so the next step is to add your friends as buddies (buddies are just what Apple calls people you chat with), and then your buddies will appear listed in your Buddy List window. Now, to add a buddy, you'll need their .Mac, or AIM, or Google Talk, etc., user-name (not their password, just their username), so your first step is to send an email to (or call) the friends you want to chat with and have them give you their usernames. Let's say for example, that one of your friends is a .Mac member, and they give you their .Mac member name. To add them as a buddy, click-and-hold on the + (plus sign) button at the bottom-left corner of your Buddy List window and choose Add Buddy from the pop-up menu that appears. A dialog will pop down where you can enter their account name, and you'll also have the choice of adding them to a group (you can have groups of co-workers, family members, friends, etc., and groups are just to help you stay organized, in case you wind up with a lot of buddies). Lastly, enter their first and last names in the fields below, and click the Add button to add your buddy. You can continue this process and add as many buddies as you'd like. Also, if you click on the little downward-facing arrow button to the right of the Last Name field, the dialog expands downward to let you choose people directly from your Address Book (of course, this only works if you entered their .Mac member name or AIM username in your Address Book in the first place, but if you did, this saves time).

Finding Out Who's Available to Chat

Once you're done adding buddies, now it's time to see who's available for chatting. You'll know that a buddy is available for a chat in two ways: (1) their name will appear under one of the three default groups (Buddies [friends], Family, or Co-Workers), and (2) there will be a green dot in front of their name, which means they're available to chat. If your buddy doesn't have iChat open, which means they're not available for chatting, their name will appear under the Offline group at the bottom. So, how does your Mac determine if your buddies are available for chatting? Actually, it doesn't— your friends choose whether they're available or not (as you'll see on the next page), and your Mac just relays that message right there in the Buddy List window. In the example above, my buddy Terry White still has iChat open, but he stepped away from his computer for a moment, so he chose Away as his iChat status. If he had closed iChat, then he would have moved to the Offline group.

Letting Your Buddies Know If You Can Chat

If you've opened up iChat, and you're available for a chat, you can let your buddies know by setting your iChat status. You do this from a pop-up menu in the upper-left corner of the Buddy List window (right under where your username is displayed, as shown here). There are already some default status messages in this list, and if you choose one, the person who sees your name in their Buddy List window will see that status. Choosing a message with a green dot in front of it tells people you're available for an iChat; a red dot means you're not available, and they won't be able to contact you if you choose a red dot (unavailable) status. Besides those default available/un-available choices, you can create your own custom message: Choose either Custom Available or Custom Away from this menu, and a text field appears where the menu used to be. Whatever you type in that field will appear beneath your name when they see you in their Buddy List window. If you don't want anyone to know you have iChat open, choose Invisible from this pop-up menu.

Actually Carrying On a Text Chat

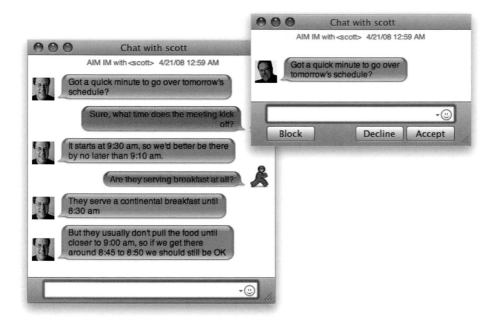

So, let's say you see a friend who's available for a text chat (their name appears under one of your groups, and it has a green dot in front of it). To send them an instant message, double-click on their name. A little window will appear, and in the field at the bottom, you can type in a text message. When you're done typing, hit the Return key on your keyboard, and a little window will pop up on your buddy's screen telling them you're trying to send them a message. If they click anywhere on that little window, their window expands, it displays your instant message (which is what you see above right), and a text field appears for them to text back to you. At that point, they can click the Accept button to start chatting with you, or they can click the Decline button, which removes the window from their screen, but just kind of leaves you hanging with no response from them (which is, I guess, better than hearing that your invitation has been declined, eh?). As you chat back and forth, your conversation is displayed on-screen using talk bubbles (as shown above left), so it visually looks like a conversation.

Doing an Audio (Voice) Chat

If you see a green telephone icon to the far right of your buddy's name (as shown above left), that means you can do an audio chat with that person (provided, of course, that you have a newer iMac, MacBook, MacBook Pro, or MacBook Air—all of which have a built-in microphone. Be sure it's turned on by selecting it from your System Preferences under Sound). Just click on the telephone icon and it invites them to an audio chat (the window you see above right pops up and they'll hear a ringing sound like a phone). If they accept, you'll see this and you can just start talking. If they don't, it does tell you across the bottom of your Audio Chat dialog that they've declined your invitation. Now, if you see a green video camera icon next to their name in your Buddy List window instead of the telephone, it means they're available for a video chat (see Chapter 7 for how to do video chats).

X MacTip: About to Send Them an Email? Wouldn't Chatting Be Faster?

If you're about to send a friend an email, before you send it, take a look in your main Mail window. If you see an email from them in your Inbox, take a look for a green dot beside their name. If you see one, that means that they're available for an iChat, so instead of emailing them, just launch iChat right now and send them an instant message.

More Mail Tips

MacTip: Bullet Points

If you need to add a bullet-point list to your email message, go under Mail's Format menu, under Lists, and choose Insert Bulleted List. Now when you type, it indents your text and adds a bullet point before each new line. When you're done with your bullet points, press the Return key twice.

MacTip: Getting Emailed Photos into iPhoto

If you want to quickly get photos that have been emailed to you imported into iPhoto, click on the message, then press Command-Y to open the attachments in Quick Look, and then click on the Add to iPhoto button in the bottom-right corner of the Quick Look window.

MacTip: Assign Email Priority the Easy Way

If you wind up assigning priorities to your emails a lot (like High Priority or Low Priority), you can add a priority pop-up menu to your New Message windows. Create a new blank email message, and to the left of the From field (your email address), you'll see a little rectangular-shaped button. Click on it, and a menu pops up. Choose Priority Field from the menu, and this adds a Priority pop-up menu to the middle-right side of your email message window.

MacTip: Sending Contacts Via Email

If you want to email someone the contact info of a person in your Address Book, just create a new email message, then go under the Window menu and choose Address Panel. Use the Search field in the top-right corner to find the person's name, and once it appears, just click on the address card icon that appears before their name, and drag-and-drop it into your email message.

MacTip: Save Time By Saving Your Favorite Templates

If you look through the templates and find some you think you'll be using from time to time, you can drag-and-drop them up onto the word "Favorites" in the list of categories on the left side. Now all your favorite email templates are just one click away.

More Mail Tips

X MacTip: Checking Spelling in Your Email

You can turn a spelling checker on for your email by going under the Mail menu and choosing Preferences. When the Mail preferences dialog appears, click on the Composing icon up top, and then from the Check Spelling pop-up menu, choose whether you want to have it check your spelling as you type, before you send the email, or choose Never if you want the spelling checker turned off. When the spelling checker is turned on, words Mail thinks are misspelled will appear underlined in red. If you highlight the word and then Control-click (or Right-click) on it, a contextual menu of suggested spellings will appear. To choose one, click on it from the menu.

X MacTip: Save Time When Creating New Email Messages

If you're working in another program, and you need to create a quick email message, try this: Control-click (or Right-click) on the Mail icon in the Dock, and from the pop-up menu that appears, choose Compose New Message, and it opens a new email message for you.

X MacTip: Getting Better Search Results in Mail

If you're searching for an email message you sent or received (using the Search field in the upper-right corner), by default it searches the Entire Message field, but don't forget about the buttons that appear at the top of the main window when you search, which let you change how the Search field searches. So you can change your search to From if you want to see only messages from Apple, instead of also seeing messages that you sent to Apple or that include the word "Apple" in the Subject line.

X MacTip: Creating Your Own iChat Groups

You can create your own custom groups by choosing Add Group from the same pop-up menu where you add buddies. Also, once you've created a buddy, if you want to assign that buddy to a particular group, you can just drag-and-drop that buddy onto the group you want them to appear within, right in the Buddy List window.

Chapter Six

Music and Your Mac

**You Can Do More Than Just Listen to Music;
You Can Make It, Too**

In most of the books I've written (nearly 50 of them now), I've followed the tradition of naming my chapter titles after either a song, a band, a TV show, or a movie that relates to the topic of the chapter—it has been the subtitle below it that really explains what the chapter is about. But in this book, I decided to keep things simple and just call 'em what they are. So, first you might be wondering why I would do that. You see, in computer books, there's not a lot of room to inject any humor, or writing style, or punctuation, or other meaningless things like that, and writing short introductions that adequately set up the material in the chapter that follows is actually pretty hard. So, I had a decision to make: (a) write meaningful intros that would prepare the reader for the chapter to come, or (b) have some fun. I figured that if you bought a Mac, you're a fairly sophisticated person, and if I had a chapter named "Music and Your Mac," you'd be able to pretty much figure out what that chapter would entail, without me having to tell you, "Hey, this chapter is about how to play music and make music." First graders would be able to figure that out, so instead, I opted for fun—I would use those TV show or song names for chapter titles, and I tried to find titles that kind of matched what the chapters here are about. For example, in my book, *The iPod Book*, for the chapter on how to work all the buttons and dials on the outside of the iPod, I named the chapter "The Outsiders" (a tribute to the 1960s band of the same name, who had a huge hit with the song "Time Won't Let Me"), and for the chapter on using the iPod video features, I named it "Video Killed the Radio Star" (from the hit song by the Buggles). So, why did I decide to dispense with those clever titles for this book? Because it was really hard coming up with songs that started with "i" (iCal, iTunes, iMovie, etc.).

Playing an Audio CD on Your Mac

If you want to play an audio CD on your Mac, just pop a CD in your Mac's disc drive, and it launches Apple's iTunes software. A dialog will appear asking you if you want to import the music tracks into iTunes. In this case, you just want to play the CD using iTunes, and not actually copy the tracks from the CD onto your Mac, so click the No button (as shown here). When you inserted the CD, iTunes quickly went and checked an online database to find the names and order of the tracks on the CD, and it displays them in the main window (the tracks shown here are from Ciara's CD, *The Evolution*). To play all the tracks in order, just double-click on track 1. To play any individual track, just double-click directly on it, but when that track is over, it will automatically play the next song in the track list, and so on, until it reaches the last track. If you want to skip a track (you don't want to hear it), just turn off the checkbox right before its name. Up in the top-left corner of the screen are the standard Rewind, Play, and Fast Forward buttons (to hear the track again, play/pause the current track, or jump to the next track in the list). When you're done listening to the CD, you can eject it by clicking the Eject button in the bottom-right corner of the iTunes window.

Getting Music onto Your Mac from a CD

Any time you insert an audio CD into your Mac's disc drive, it's going to ask whether you want to import the CD or not. On the previous page, we skipped the importing, and just played the CD as if our Mac was a just a CD music player. However, if you want to be able to play the tracks on that CD without actually having the CD inserted into your Mac's disc drive, then you'll need to import the CD (this copies the music into your iTunes Music library). So, when that little dialog appears (when you first insert a CD) that asks if you want to import the songs on the CD, click the Yes button. If you've already clicked No, it's not too late—just click the Import CD button in the bottom-right corner of the iTunes window (as shown here). This starts the importing process, and you can see the progress of the songs being imported in the info window at the top of the iTunes window. While a track is being downloaded, it has a spinning little yellow icon before the track's name. When the track is fully imported, that icon turns green. To skip importing a track you don't want on your Mac, just turn off the checkbox before the track's name. Once all the tracks you want are imported, the songs are now in iTunes (and on your Mac), so you can eject the disc by clicking the Eject button in the bottom-right corner.

⚠ MacTip: Automatically Importing Any CD You Insert

If you always want music from CDs imported, go to iTunes' Preferences (under the iTunes menu), click on the Advanced tab, then on the Importing tab, and for On CD Insert, choose Import CD and Eject.

Finding Music in the iTunes Store

The most popular online music store in the world is Apple's history-making iTunes Store (which now offers everything from downloadable feature-length Hollywood movies to music videos and TV shows, and you can rent movies, as well). Buying music couldn't be easier—you start by clicking on the iTunes Store link in the Source list on the left side of the iTunes window (the iTunes Store is an online store, so I probably don't need to say this, but…you know you need to be online to access an online store, right? Okay, sorry, I had to). You start at the iTunes Store homepage, and if you just want to see the music part of the iTunes Store, click on the Music link at the top left of the Store's homepage, which takes you to the homepage for music. You can browse for music, but honestly, the quickest way to get to the songs you want is to use the Search field up in the top-right corner. Just type in the name of the song (or the artist, or album, etc.) and it will bring up a list of matching songs (artists, albums, etc.). It does an amazingly good job of searching, and if the iTunes Store carries the song you're looking for, you'll find it (and since it carries literally millions of songs, chances are it's there). By the way, you can hear a 30-second preview of any song by simply double-clicking on the song. (I use these previews to make sure that the version of the song I want is the right one before I buy it. That way I don't wind up with an unplugged, extended, or concert version of the song accidentally when I was looking for the original studio track.)

Buying Songs from the iTunes Store

When you find the song you're looking for in the iTunes Store, you can buy it (which downloads the song to your computer so you can play it anytime, or copy it over to your iPod or iPhone). Just click on the Buy Song button that appears on the far-right side of the song's listing (it's circled here in red), and the song starts downloading immediately (if you're logged into your account. Before you download your first song, you'll have to set up an account with the iTunes Store—it just takes a few moments, and a credit card, of course). Once a song is downloaded (they download surprisingly quickly), you can find it by clicking on the Purchased link on the left side of the iTunes window. The last song in the list is the last song you purchased.

Getting Other Music into iTunes

If you already have music on your Mac (maybe you downloaded it from a band's website), you can get that music into iTunes by simply dragging-and-dropping it right onto the iTunes icon in the Dock. It imports the song into iTunes and adds it to your Music library.

Making a Playlist of Your Favorite Songs

Once you've bought songs or imported songs from CDs, the next thing you'll want to do is create playlists of your favorite songs. For example, if you've imported three CDs of Red Hot Chili Peppers songs, you might want to put them into a playlist (kind of like a folder), so when you're in the mood to hear some Chili Peppers, you'll just click on that playlist and it will play just their songs. Or you might want to have a playlist of "big hair" bands of the 80s (like I do), or a playlist of road trip songs, or party songs, or...well, that's half of the fun of this—creating your own custom playlists. To make a playlist, just click the Create a Playlist button (it's the little plus sign) in the bottom-left corner of the iTunes window. This adds a new playlist to the Source list on the left side of the window, and its name is already highlighted so you can type one in. Type in a name, press the Return key, then click on Music (at the top of that list on the left side) to see your whole Music library. To add songs to your playlist, just drag-and-drop them right onto that playlist. To remove a song from a playlist, just click on it, then press the Delete key on your keyboard (by the way, deleting a song from a playlist doesn't remove it from your main Music library, it just removes it from that playlist, so you can add and delete songs from playlists without worrying about messing with the original song files). To delete an entire playlist, just click on it and press the Delete key on your keyboard (again, removing a playlist doesn't remove the songs from your main library, it just deletes the playlist itself).

Getting Music from Your Mac onto an iPod

If you have an iPod (or an iPhone, which has an iPod built right in), getting songs from iTunes onto your iPod couldn't be easier. Get the white USB cable that came with your iPod and connect one end to your iPod. Plug the other end into a USB port on your Mac, and it syncs the two—all the music and playlists you have in iTunes will be copied over to your iPod. Once the syncing is complete (look at the screen on your iPod and it will say "Connected. Eject Before Disconnecting"), you can click the little Eject icon next to your iPod in the iTunes Source list, unplug your iPod, and start listening. The cool thing is, from this point on, any changes you make in iTunes will automatically be updated in your iPod the next time you connect it to your Mac (so if you create new playlists, or edit existing playlists, or buy more songs, etc., it will automatically sync right up—all you have to do is plug it in).

Hearing a Song Without iTunes

If you want to hear a song without importing it into iTunes, just click on the song file in a Finder window, then hit the Spacebar on your keyboard. This opens the Quick Look window and starts playing the song. There's even a "scrubber bar" (click-and-drag it to move forward or backward in the song), and a Pause/Play button. If the song includes embedded album artwork, you see that, too.

Burning an Audio CD

If you've got a playlist you'd like to have as an audio CD, just click on the playlist (in the Source list on the left of the iTunes window), then click the Burn Disc button in the bottom-right corner of the iTunes window (as shown above). iTunes will ask you to "Insert a blank disc," so…insert a blank disc, and it takes it from there. When you're done, the songs are burned onto a CD you can eject and play on regular CD players (like the one in your car). One thing to note that only applies to playing this audio CD on computers: if your CD contains songs you bought from the iTunes Store (most of which have built-in copy protection), you'll only be able to play this CD on computers that you've authorized to play protected music (you can authorize up to five computers). Again, this doesn't affect playing the CD in your car or on your stereo—just on computers.

Using External Speakers with Your Mac

If you're seriously into music on your Mac, you're seriously going to want to get some better (bigger) audio speakers than the ones that come with your Mac (I really like the M-Audio Studiophile AV 40 Speaker System, for around $150, and you can find them on Apple's website in their online store. They're amazing). Connecting external speakers is easy—you just use a ⅛" stereo cord, and connect one end to your Mac's audio-out port (that place where you'd plug in headphones), the other end to the speaker's ⅛" stereo input (those M-Audio speakers I just mentioned have that input right on the front), and you're set.

Recording Music on Your Mac

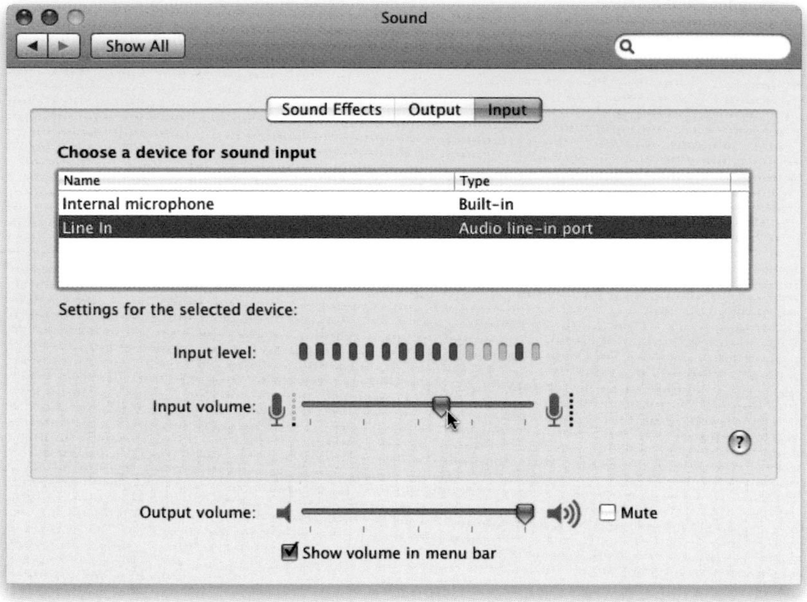

Sound

Show All

Sound Effects | **Output** | **Input**

Choose a device for sound input

Name	Type
Internal microphone	Built-in
Line In	Audio line-in port

Settings for the selected device:

Input level: ▮▮▮▮▮▮▮▮▮▮▮▯▯▯▯▯

Input volume:

Output volume: ☐ Mute

☑ Show volume in menu bar

If you want to record audio on your Mac (maybe transferring it from a cassette player or another audio source), there's a ⅛" stereo audio-in port on your Mac for doing just that. Just plug the cable into that port (it's right next to the headphone port), then go under the Apple menu and choose System Preferences. When the System Preferences dialog appears, click on Sound, then click on the Input tab at the top, and then where it says "Choose a device for sound input," click on Line In, which selects your Mac's audio line-in port (as seen above). The slider below that determines what the level (volume) of the audio signal coming into your Mac will be (you don't want it too high, or it will start to distort). When you start your audio playing, you'll see the meter above the slider start to move, so just make sure that when the music is at its loudest point, it's not anywhere near hitting the far-right edge of the meter. That's pretty much all there is to it. By the way, if you connect your audio source using a USB cable (like a USB-based microphone for recording), you'll see the USB-based audio input appear in the list separately, and you can just click on that directly to choose it.

Making Your Own Music with GarageBand

Every Mac these days comes with GarageBand, which is amazing, because GarageBand is a surprisingly sophisticated, yet surprisingly easy-to-use, built-in recording studio and music track creation tool, all in one (it's so good, there are professional recording studios that use it as their main digital recording software tool). But beyond being this really clever, well-designed, powerful "music studio," it's just plain fun. Even if you have no musical background, you'll be able to make music (using the pre-recorded "loops" it comes with). First, you'll find GarageBand in your Applications folder, so go there and launch it now (oh, come on, take a couple of minutes and have some fun, will ya?). I'm just going to turn you on to GarageBand here, and on the next few pages, with a really simple project, but if you stick with me for just a few minutes, I promise you'll have a blast. When you launch GarageBand, a splash screen appears asking what you want to do. Click the Create New Music Project button and the New Project dialog appears (shown above). You don't have to do anything here (the default settings are fine, unless you want to name your song now), so just click Create, and on the next page, the fun begins.

X MacTip: You Can Edit the Tempo, Key, Etc., Later

Don't worry about making the wrong choices here, in this New Project dialog—you can always change these settings later (see the tip two pages ahead).

Using the Built-In Pre-Recorded Music Tracks

When GarageBand opens, you'll see a little floating keyboard in the middle of the screen. Take two seconds and click on the keys, and you'll hear a pretty darn nice quality piano sound as you hit each key. Now, take your cursor, hold it on a key, and run it up and down the keyboard. Kinda cool, but at this point, we don't need it for what we're going to do, so click the round red Close button in the top-left corner of the keyboard. Now, inside GarageBand are all these pre-recorded music tracks called loops that repeat over and over as many times as you want (I'm talking drum tracks, bass tracks, guitar tracks, horns—you name it), and you're going to create songs (perfect as royalty-free background music for videos or slide shows) by simply dragging-and-dropping these loops (it's way cooler than it sounds). To find this library of loops, click on the Loop Browser button (it looks like an eye) in the bottom-left corner (shown circled here in red), and a dialog will pop up, letting you know that there are *tons* more loops you can download for free from Apple, but you're going to skip that for now, and just work with the ones that are already installed on your Mac (although at some point, once you're hooked on GarageBand, you'll probably want more loops, so you can go download them then). For now, just close that dialog, and let's get to loopin'.

Adding Drums to Your Song
(Hey, It's a Start)

When the Loop Browser pops up from the bottom of the screen, click on the Kits button for a selection of pre-recorded tracks using drum kits. In the Name field on the right, scroll down to Live Edgy Drums 03 (as seen here) and click on it to hear a preview of how the drum loop sounds (to stop the preview, just click on it again). Now, drag-and-drop that loop up onto the music Timeline up top (as shown here) to place it into your song. By default, this drum track will play for four measures, but if you want it to go longer, just put your cursor over the top half of the top-right corner of that blue bar that represents the drum track, and your cursor will change into a circular arrow. Click-and-drag out that track for as long as you want it to repeat (for now just drag it out through 12 full measures). Now hit the Start/Stop Playback button (right below the Timeline, and just above the Loop Browser) to hear the track play for 12 measures (also called "bars"). On the next page, we'll add more instrument tracks.

X MacTip: Changing Your Tempo, Key, or Time Signature

If you want to change the tempo (speed) of your song, go under the Control menu and choose Show Tempo in LCD. Now, the current tempo will appear in the LCD right above the Loop Browser, and if you click on it, a pop-up slider will appear so you can adjust the tempo. There are also key controls (to the left of the tempo control) and time signature controls (to the right of it). Click on either to adjust them.

Adding the Bass Track

Now let's add some bass. To leave the drum kit loops, click on Kits again, and now you can choose a new category of instruments. Click on Bass, over on the far-left side of the window, then in the list of loops, scroll down and click on Electric Slap 02, and drag that up onto your Timeline. Once again, click on the top half of the far-right side of the blue track in the Timeline and drag it out until it reaches 13 bars (as shown here, where you can see the little circular loop icon). Now press the Return key (shortcut for rewinding to the beginning of the song) and listen to your track. Kinda "Old School," ain't it? (You know what they say: "There's no school like the old school.") Anyway, that's the process: you find a loop you like, drag it up onto the Timeline, and hit the Start/Stop Playback button (by the way, it's easier just to press the Spacebar on your keyboard, which is the shortcut for the Start/Stop Playback button).

X MacTip: How to Delete Tracks—and Other Stuff You'll Want to Know

To delete a music track you don't want (like the Bass or a Synth), just click on the track, then press Command-Delete on your keyboard. To duplicate a track, press Command-D (this gives you an empty track with that instrument—it doesn't copy the loop itself, but it saves time because now all you have to do is choose a loop from the scrolling list). If you want to move multiple tracks, Shift-click on them to select them—now you can make your song longer by just dragging the top end of any one track to the right.

Adding Keyboards and Saving Your Song

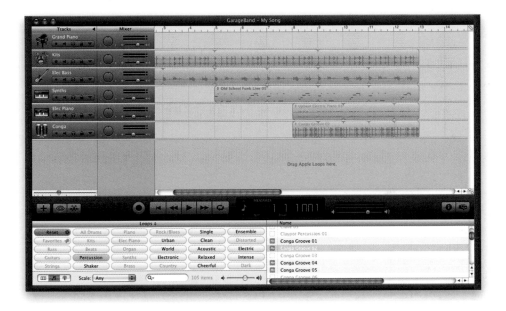

Let's add two or three more tracks, because we're going to do some arranging and mixing (it's easier than it sounds). Click on the Bass button in the Loop Browser to deselect it. Now click on Synths, and then scroll down and choose Old School Funk Line 05, but instead of just clicking-and-dragging it up to the Timeline at the beginning of the song (like we've been doing), when you drag it up there, drag it over so it starts at measure 5 (look up above the Timeline to see which measure is which). That way, the drums and bass play for four bars by themselves, and then the synthesizer comes in. Don't forget to drag out the green Synths track through the twelfth bar (as shown here), then rewind, hit the Spacebar, and soak in the funk (so to speak). Now, to me, the Synths track seems a little bit loud, but you can control the volume of each track individually in the mixer on left side of each track. Just let your song play and, when the synth kicks in, drag the volume slider to the right until it blends in better with the volume of the bass and drums. If you want, finish things off by adding two more tracks: (1) Electric Piano section, Up-beat Electric Piano 03, and add it starting at measure 8, and (2) click on Percussion and choose Conga Groove 02, and add it starting at measure 8, as well, but then adjust the volume down a bit. When you're done, you can use it as background music for a slide show, or a movie, etc. Just go up under GarageBand's Share menu, and you can choose to send the completed song to iTunes, or over to iWeb for posting it on a webpage, or you can burn the song to CD. See, I told you this would be fun.

More Tips for Music on Your Mac

X MacTip: Making Your iTunes Font Size Bigger

The default type size in iTunes is pretty small, and if you want a larger font size, go under the iTunes menu and choose Preferences, then click on the General icon. There are two pop-up menus at the top: one for Source Text (the menus and such) and one for Song Text (the text you see in your playlists and library). To make your font sizes bigger, choose Large from the pop-up menus.

X MacTip: Printing Album Cover Jewel Cases for Your CDs Right Out of iTunes

Click on the playlist you burned to CD, then go under the File menu and choose Print. In the Print dialog, under Print, choose CD Jewel Case Insert. iTunes automatically creates a list of the songs and their running times, and there's a pop-up menu where you can choose from a selection of themes for your insert, including ones with multiple or single album covers.

X MacTip: Making iTunes Take Up Less Space

Once your music is playing, you can click once on the green + (plus sign) button in the upper-left corner of the iTunes window to shrink iTunes down to a mini-player that takes up a lot less space (but you still have access to the Play, Rewind, Fast Forward, and Volume buttons). To return to full size, just click the green button again.

X MacTip: Why You Need to Back Up Your Purchased Songs

If your hard drive dies, all of your purchased songs go right to the grave with it. Apple will not let you download them again without paying for them. That's why it's SO important to back up your purchased music. To do this, first click on Purchased in the Source list (on the left side of the iTunes window) to select it. Then click on the Burn Disc button in the bottom right-hand corner of the iTunes window. Insert a blank disc (when iTunes tells you to), then start-a-burnin'. Keep poppin' in new discs until all those songs are backed up to CD.

X MacTip: Changing Volume from Your Keyboard

To increase the volume while you're playing a song in iTunes, press Command-Up Arrow and to turn it back down, press Command-Down Arrow.

More Tips for Music on Your Mac

X MacTip: Automatic Authorizing

Authorizing is an automatic thing: if you plug in your iPod to another one of your computers (like a laptop for instance), a dialog appears letting you know that this isn't an authorized computer, but as long as you haven't used up your five-computer limit, it will allow you to authorize that computer right there on the spot. Feel the power!

X MacTip: Make Your Music Sound Better Using the Built-In EQ

By default, iTunes sets your bass and treble controls to zero, which to most folks sounds kind of flat. So, to make your music sound dramatically better, turn on the iTunes built-in graphic equalizer (EQ) presets. Go under the View menu and choose Show Equalizer. At the top, just choose the type of music you're listening to, and iTunes creates an EQ setting to make your music sound its best.

X MacTip: Get a Bigger Keyboard in GarageBand

That little built-in keyboard that appears onscreen in GarageBand is just that—little. If you want a full 88-key keyboard (like a real piano), click the green zoom button in the upper-left corner (or click-and-drag out the bottom-right corner), and it expands to a much larger size.

X MacTip: Using GarageBand's Built-In Tuner

If you're plugging other instruments into your Mac (like an electric guitar or bass), so you can play along or record them using iTunes, you'll be happy to know there's a built-in tuner. First create a new Real Instrument track, then click on the little icon that appears on the far left of the LCD window and choose Tuner.

X MacTip: Five GarageBand Keyboard Shortcuts You'll Want to Know

(1) To temporarily mute any track, click on it and press the letter M. (2) Pressing the Spacebar starts/stops your song. (3) Press S to hear only the currently selected track (it mutes all the other tracks for you). (4) Press the letter R to start recording. And, (5) press C to turn looping on/off.

Chapter Seven

Playing and Making Videos on Your Mac

Your Mac Is Half Movie Theater, Half Movie Studio. Here's How to Use Both

Anytime I want to show off my Mac to a PC user, the first thing I show them is how crazy easy it is to make a movie. This usually blows them away, because in most cases, it's easier to squeeze toothpaste back into the tube than it is to make a simple home movie on a PC. Now, I'm not talking about video professionals here, who are quite accustomed to using and cussing PCs—I'm talking regular, everyday people who shoot video of their kid's dance recital, or their son's birthday party, and they just want to edit a few clips, add a title or two, and save It to a DVD. These people are hosed, because on a PC there are three very distinct groups of people engaged in the video process: (1) people who've managed to figure out how to get video onto their PC, but who have no hope whatsoever of actually editing that video; (2) people who've imported some video, and somehow figured out the Byzantine labyrinth of sliders, knobs, and dials required to make even the simplest of video edits; and (3) that rare user (whose day job is probably in IT at a large company), who is one of the few people on earth who have figured out not only how to import and edit video on a PC, they've learned one of the last remaining mysteries of modern day man, which is how to get video out of a PC onto a DVD. This person is in such demand by friends, co-workers, school districts, and so on, that it's unlikely they'll be able to take as much as a bathroom break until 2011. But for Mac users like yourself, video is just a thing we do. It's how we roll. It's how our shizzles go fazizzle (by the way, I have no idea what that means, but I figure if I don't know, there's no way my editors know, because they're still feelin' the old school flavas).

Watching a DVD on Your Mac

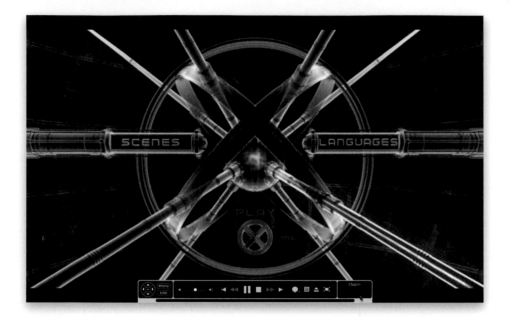

You can play standard DVD movies on your Mac, and use it just like any regular stand-alone DVD player. You just insert the movie's DVD into your Mac's disc drive, and then your Mac kicks into Full Screen mode and starts playing the DVD. You can get to the controls for pausing, jumping to the next chapter, etc., by moving your mouse to the bottom of the screen, and the Controller Bar will pop up (as seen above). There are standard navigation controls for moving around the screen on the left side of the Controller Bar, but one of the advantages of watching DVDs on a Mac is you've got a mouse (or a trackpad), and you can just move your cursor right where you want it and click. The other standard control buttons are here, too, and if you want to know which button does what, just pause your cursor over any of them, and a little description will pop up. When you're done with these controls, just move your cursor away from the Controller Bar and it tucks back away.

Watching Videos Using the QuickTime Player

PhotoshopUser TV Episode 124 (March 10, 2008)

If you want to play a video that's already on your Mac, just double-click on it, and chances are it will open in the QuickTime Player (this makes sense, since the format for video on the Mac Is Apple's QuickTime). If, for some reason, it doesn't automatically open the QuickTime Player, then just drag-and-drop the movie directly onto the Quick-Time Player icon in your Dock (or in your Applications folder).

Watching Movies Using Quick Look

Want to watch a video right now? Just click on it and press the Spacebar, and your movie will open in Quick Look and start playing. Although it's the absolute fastest way to start watching a movie (because no player application has to load—it just pops up and starts playing), it's pretty much a bare-bones video player—its only controls are a scrubber bar, volume control, Full Screen button, and a Play/Pause button.

X MacTip: Previewing Movies in Column View

If you use Column view when you're in a Finder window, here's a really cool tip: When you see a movie file, you can see a preview of the movie right there in the Finder window, without even opening Quick Look. Just click on the video file, and the info on the file, along with the first frame, appears in the far-right column. Move your cursor over that first frame, and a Play/Pause button appears in the center of it—click on it to start the preview. Click again to stop the preview.

How to Get a Video on YouTube.com

YouTube™ **Publish your project to YouTube**

Account: skelby Add... Remove

Category: Comedy

Title: Behind the Scenes at Photoshop User TV

Description: A look behind the scenes during a taping of Photoshop User TV, featuring "The Photoshop Guys: Dave Cross, Matt Kloskowski, and Scott Kelby."

Tags: Photoshop, Adobe, Tutorials

iPhone ￼tv Computer YouTube

Size to publish: ● Mobile ● ● ● 480x272 ￼
○ Medium ● ● ● 640x360 ￼

☐ Make this movie private

Cancel Next

If you want to make a video that will get posted on YouTube.com, use iMovie to make your movie (turn to page 156 for a couple quick tutorials on the basics of creating movies in iMovie), and then when your movie is done, go under iMovie's Share menu and choose YouTube. The dialog you see above will appear. Click the Add button to sign in to your YouTube account (of course, if you don't have an account, you'll have to create one, but luckily, it's free and you can do that here). Click the Sign In button and you'll be taken to YouTube.com where you'll sign in or create your account. You'll then have to give YouTube.com your permission for your movies to be posted to your account from right within iMovie. Click the Allow button, close the YouTube.com Safari window, and once you're back in iMovie, click the Confirm Sign In button. You can now add your title, description, search tags (so people can find your video), and choose a size to publish, then click the Next button. The next panel just confirms that you want to publish your movie to YouTube. Click the Publish button, and iMovie uploads your movie to your YouTube.com account for you. Yes, it's that easy.

Watching Video Using Front Row

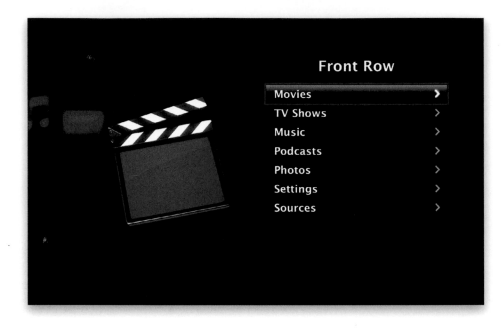

If you want to use your Mac as a digital theater, try watching your movies using your Mac's remote and Front Row. Using Front Row, you can watch any of the videos you've down-loaded from the iTunes Store, imported into iTunes, or just any movies you have in your Mac's Movies folder. To enter Front Row, press Command-Esc, and when the Front Row interface appears, use the Up/Down Arrow keys to navigate to Movies, and then press the Return key on your keyboard (or if you're using an Apple Remote, use the + [plus sign] or – [minus sign] buttons to navigate and then press the Play/Pause button). This takes you to the main Movies screen, where you can watch previews of movies or any movies from iTunes, or use the Up/Down Arrow keys on your keyboard to scroll down to your Movies Folder, and then choose movies from there. When you're done, press the Esc key to return to the previous window, and press it three times to leave Front Row altogether.

X **MacTip: Playing DVDs in Front Row**

Since there's no DVD option in the Front Row menu, you're probably wondering if you can play DVDs at all. Yes, you can, but you don't see the DVD option until you actually have a DVD inserted into your Mac's disc drive. So, insert a disc, then enter Front Row, and you'll see it as one of your options.

Doing a One-on-One Video Chat

If you have an iMac, MacBook, MacBook Pro, or MacBook Air, you have a video camera built right into your monitor, which means you can do video chats—where you see the person you're chatting with and they can see you, too (if you have a high-speed Internet connection. If you're using dial-up, you'll be sticking to text chats). I'm assuming (at this point) that you've read how to set up iChat to do regular text chatting (if not, see Chapter 5), so here we're just going to look at video chatting. The way to know if someone in your iChat buddy list is available and able to have a video chat is to: (1) Look to the left of their name, and if you see a little green dot, they are available. (2) Look to the right of their name, and if you see a green camera icon, they have a video camera connected and could chat with you (if they accept your invitation, but seriously, who wouldn't want to chat with you, really cool person who bought my book? Exactly). Double-click on their green camera icon and a video window will appear that shows you what your camera is seeing (that's you, by the way), and a window appears on the other person's Mac inviting them to a video chat. If they click anywhere in this window it expands to show a video window (as you see on the right here), and if they click the Accept button at the bottom to accept your invitation, your video chat begins. If at any time you don't want the other person to see you (you suddenly spot a piece of spinach in your teeth and quickly need to eradicate it), you can freeze and mute your video by Option-clicking on the microphone button at the bottom of the window. When you're done, and ready to resume the video chat, just click on that microphone button again and your video goes live again.

Doing a Three–Way Video Chat

You can have up to four people chatting in the same video chat—just send an invite to two or three people (maximum) by double-clicking on their green video icons. As they accept, they'll join the chat, and all of your screens will be displayed in the iChat video window (it's pretty much like a conference call, but with video).

Buying Movies Online

You can buy full-length Hollywood movies from Apple's iTunes Store, and watch them full screen right on your Mac within iTunes, or you can watch them within Front Row, or you can copy them onto your iPod or iPhone and watch them there. It all starts in iTunes, so launch that first (click on its icon in your Dock or double-click on it in your Applications folder), and then click on the iTunes Store in the Source list on the left side of the iTunes window. When the Store's homepage appears, in the list of links at the top left, click on Movies to jump to the Movies homepage. On the Movies homepage, what I usually do is scroll down to the Genres list (on the lower-left side), and click on the genre I'm looking for (like Kids & Family, or Sci-Fi & Fantasy, or Comedy, etc.) and then it takes me to the main page for that genre. Of course, if you know exactly which movie you're looking for, the quickest way to find it is to simply type its name in the Search field up in the top-right corner of the iTunes window. Once you find a movie that looks interesting, click on its cover (or if it's in a list, click on its name) and the page for that movie appears. You'll see a full description of the movie, you can watch the movie trailer, and you'll see buttons to rent or buy the movie (not all movies are available for renting, and not all of the rentals are available to buy, but you'll be able to tell at a glance by the Buy Movie and Rent Movie buttons). That's all there is to it.

Renting Movies

If you don't want to buy a movie, you can rent it for 24 hours (it downloads to your Mac, and you can watch it there, or transfer it to your iPod or iPhone and watch it there). Although the rental is for 24 hours, that 24-hour clock doesn't start ticking until you actually hit the Play button and start watching the movie—and you have 30 days from the day you download the rental to hit that Play button. As of the writing of this book, Apple charges $2.99 for renting a movie, or $3.99 for renting the high-definition version, but of course that price is subject to change at any time (you'll see the current rental price listed right on the page for the movie you're going to rent, so there won't be any surprises).

Recording Video with Your Built-In Camera

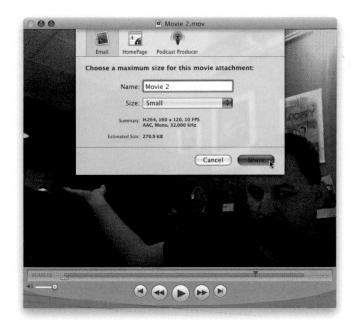

There are two ways to create movies on your Mac: one uses iMovie (more on this later in this chapter), but if you upgrade to Apple's QuickTime Pro (the upgrade costs $29.99, and to upgrade, you can choose Buy QuickTime Pro from the QuickTime Player menu), you can use it to record video clips using the built-in camera on your Mac. Here's how: Launch QuickTime Player, and then go under the File menu and choose New Movie Recording. This opens a preview window and shows you the current image your Mac's built-in camera is seeing (provided, of course, that you have an iMac, MacBook, MacBook Air, or MacBook Pro, which all have a built-in camera). There's just one button in this window—the red Record button. Click on it, and it starts recording both audio and video. When you're done recording, just click it again. If you want to email your movie to someone, go under the QuickTime Player's File menu and choose Share. When the dialog you see above pops down, click on the Email icon up top, then give your video a name, choose your size (remember, the larger the size you choose, the larger the movie's file size), and then click the Share button. It resizes and compresses the video, then launches Mail and attaches your movie to a new blank email message, ready to go. Creating videos doesn't get much faster, or easier, than that.

Getting Video into Your Mac (Using iMovie)

If you've been shooting with your own video camera, and you want to get that video onto your Mac so you can edit it, share it, etc., first you need to connect your camera to your Mac—depending on your camera type, you'll either use a FireWire cable (if your Mac has a FireWire port) or a USB cable (all Macs have USB ports). Once connected, set your camera to its playback mode and launch iMovie (it's in the Dock, or you can find it in the Applications folder). When iMovie opens, an Import From dialog pops up so you can import your video. You basically have two choices here: (1) Automatic, where you just click the Import button in the bottom-right corner of the dialog and it imports all the video you recorded, or (2) Manual, which is what I usually do, because it lets me choose just the parts of the video I want to import (that way, I'm not eating up hard drive space with video I'm never going to use, like the time I left the camera recording when I thought it was off, and I recorded 14 minutes of the ground as I walked around). To switch to Manual mode, just flip the little switch in the lower-left corner of the dialog down to Manual (as shown here), and you'll see a new set of controls appear that are like the controls on the camera itself (Rewind, Fast Forward, Stop, and Play). Click the Play button and the video on your camera starts playing. When you see a part of the video you want to import, click the Import button, and a dialog pops down (as seen above), where you can name the clip. Click OK and it starts the tape again and starts importing from that point. When you're finished importing that clip, click the Stop button. That's the process, so go ahead and start importing.

Where the Video You Imported Winds Up

Once you've imported all the video you want off your camera, click the Done button, and you'll see that the clips you just imported now appear in iMovie's source video library for that event (that wide gray area on the bottom half of the screen). This is basically where video clips sit until you're ready to use them in your movie, but while they're just sitting there, you can see a preview of each clip by simply moving your cursor over the clip's thumbnail (just move across the thumbnail, and you'll see a live preview appear up in the top-right Viewer). This is handy, because it's hard to tell what's in each clip without being able to get a quick preview, and moving your cursor across the thumbnail gives you a really quick look. If you actually want to see the whole clip, and hear the audio, just click on the thumbnail, then press the Spacebar. To stop it, press the Spacebar again.

X **MacTip: Use Events to Keep Your Videos Organized**

Once you've shot all this video from different events (like your kid's birthday party, the new building groundbreaking at church, and your daughter's dance recital), how do you keep all these different clips organized? By using Events (when you import your video and give it a name, it'll become an Event in your Event Library at the bottom left of the window). These are like folders in iMovie, and they let you stay organized by putting related videos together in one place. That way you can just click on Dance Recital, for example, and just those video clips appear in the source video library.

Putting Your Video Clips into Your Movie

When you're ready to start putting your movie together, you're going to click-and-drag clips from the source video library and drop them, in the order you want them, into the Project area (the dark gray area in the top center). But wait, you don't just click-and-drag the clips, you select which clip parts you want there first, and you click-and-drag those (after all, when you import from the camera, it's hard to be very precise, but now, when you're putting the actual movie together, it's time to "tighten things up"). So, here's how that works: You click, hold, and drag over a clip (in the source video library), and a little yellow cropping border appears. The area inside that yellow border is the part of the video you want (you see a big preview of the area you're scrubbing over in the Viewer in the top right of the iMovie window, as seen above). Once this cropping border is in place, you can edit it by grabbing one of the sides and clicking-and-dragging in either direction, and it lets you get very precise—even down to individual frames (it actually works very well). Once you have the exact part of the clip you want inside that yellow cropping border, you click on that area and drag-and-drop it up into the Project area, and that clip is now part of your movie (you can change its position later). So, that's what you do: you move your cursor over each clip, select the part you want, click-and-drag that part up to the Project area, and then name your project and choose the size. If you do want the entire clip, then click-and-drag your cursor over the entire clip to select it all, then click-and-drag it up top.

Adding Transitions to Your Movie

Your videos play in the order you see them in the Project area (from left to right), and they jump directly from clip to clip without a smooth dissolve or any transitions between the clips; it's just a cut from scene to scene. If you'd like to add a transition between clips, click on the Transitions Browser button (shown circled here), and the Transitions Browser slides out from the lower-right side of the window. To see a preview of what a transition looks like, just hover your cursor over it. To add a transition to your movie, just click-and-drag the one you want from the Transitions Browser and drop it in between the two clips where you want it, up in the Project area. That's all there is to it.

X MacTip: Adding Photos to Your Movie

If you want to add photos to your movie, just click on the Photos Browser button in the toolbar in the center of iMovie (it's the button with the camera icon to the left of the Transitions Browser button), and it slides out from the right side. This gives you access to all the photos and albums you have in iPhoto, and any photos you've created in Photo Booth. If you see a photo you want you use, just click on it and drag it up to your Project area, and it becomes part of your movie. Also, there's a search field at the bottom to help you locate just the photo you're looking for.

Adding Music to Your Movie

If you want to add a background music track to your movie, click the Music and Sound Effects Browser button in the middle-right side of the window (circled here in red) and the browser slides out from the side (as seen above). At the top of the browser, you can choose to add sound effects from iMovie's built-in collection of sound effects, or songs you've created in GarageBand, or songs you have in iTunes. Just click on the one you want, then in the list below, choose the song you want to add as a background music track. Once you've found it (you can hear a preview of any song by clicking on it, then clicking on the Play button), just drag-and-drop the song anywhere in the Project area and it's automatically added as a background track to your movie (you can see it's been added because it adds a green tinted background behind the clips in your movie and you'll see a little musical note icon at the end of the green area). Press the Spacebar to see and hear your movie. By default, the music fades at the end of the last clip, but if you'd like to choose where it fades out (or where it fades in for that matter), just click anywhere in the green area, then press Command-R to bring up the Trim Music editor. Click-and-drag the yellow bar at the end of the track to the left to have the music fade out sooner (as you drag, you'll see where you are in the song by the minutes/seconds that appear). To have the music fade in later, just click-and-drag the yellow bar at the beginning over to the right. When you're done, click the Done button at the top right of the Project area.

Putting Your Own Movies on DVD

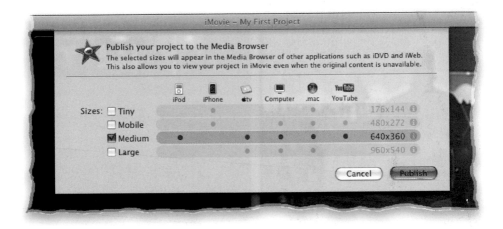

If you've created a movie using iMovie, you can burn that movie to DVD and give it to… well…whomever, but burning it to DVD isn't as obvious as you might think. First, you need to save the video to the Media Browser (so the movie you save is available to other Apple applications that can use movies as part of a project). Go under iMovie's Share menu and choose Media Browser. A dialog will pop down from the top of the iMovie window (as seen above) asking you to choose the size you want for your movie (the dialog gives you an idea of which size works best for which type of final output you're thinking about. For example, if your final movie will be shown only on Apple TV, on your computer, or posted to .Mac, it recommends saving in Large format). Once you make your choice, click the Publish button and then quit iMovie (Command-Q), because now your movie has been resized, compressed, and saved in your Mac's Media Browser. You can now launch iDVD (the program for creating DVDs on a Mac). Start by choosing a theme for your DVD from the Themes list, then click on the Media button in the bottom-right corner of the window. Click on the Movies tab at the top right, and in the list that appears, click on the movie you just published. Now, drag-and-drop it onto your iDVD theme (for more on using iDVD, see Chapter 8). Once you've edited the text in your iDVD theme, and tested the DVD to make sure it looks and works the way you want it to, click the Burn button (it's to the immediate right of the Preview DVD Playback button, at the bottom of the window) and you'll be prompted to insert a blank DVD. Once you do, it burns your movie and theme interface to the disc (I told you it wasn't real obvious). (*Note*: Your Mac must have a SuperDrive or be connected to an external DVD burner to burn DVDs.)

More Tips for Using Video on Your Mac

X MacTip: Getting Back to the Main Menu When Watching a DVD

There's a keyboard shortcut you can use any time to get back to your DVDs Main Menu: it's Command-D.

X MacTip: Quickly Hiding the DVD Controller

If you press Command-Option-C, it quickly hides the DVD Player Controller Bar from view. Press it again to bring it back.

X MacTip: Recording Video Straight from Your Camera to QuickTime

If you want to create really simple video, you can just connect a digital video camera to your Mac (using a FireWire or USB cable), and then record that video using QuickTime Pro. Just set your camera to Record mode and launch the Quick-Time Pro Player. Then choose New Movie Recording from the File menu, and you'll see a preview of what your camera is capturing (if you don't see a preview, go to QuickTime Player's preferences and make sure your camera is selected in the Recording pane). Press the red Record button to start capturing that video onto your Mac.

X MacTip: Sharing Your Movies

Besides burning movies to DVD, you can export your movie (under iMovie's Share menu) as a stand-alone movie you can email to other people, post on the Web, etc. For more advanced export choices, choose Export as QuickTime, instead.

X MacTip: Doing Video Chats with Your Own Digital Video Camera

If you don't have a built-in video camera on your Mac, but you want to do video chats using iChat, you can use a standard digital video camcorder instead. Just use a DV-to-FireWire connector to connect your DV camcorder to your Mac, then launch iChat and it will see your camera and you're off and running. One more tip: to keep your camera from automatically going to sleep (which is a common feature on most DV camcorders), just remove the tape before you start your iChat.

More Tips for Using Video on Your Mac

MacTip: Recording from Your Mac's Built-In Camera

If you have QuickTime Pro, you can not only record video straight from your digital video camcorder right onto your Mac, but you can also record right off your Mac's built-in iSight camera (if you have a Mac with a built-in camera, of course). Start by launching QuickTime Pro, then go under the QuickTime Player menu and choose Preferences. In the Preferences dialog, click on the Recording icon at the top and the recording preferences appear, where you can choose which audio and video source you want to record with.

MacTip: Tweaking Your Movies Right in QuickTime Pro

If you want to adjust the tint, color, brightness, or contrast of your video, just open it in QuickTime Pro and then press Command-K to bring up the floating A/V Controls editing palette, where you can adjust these aspects to your heart's content. Also, feel free to experiment with different looks, because you can return to the original by clicking the Reset button.

MacTip: Watching DVDs in a Floating Window

If you don't want to watch your DVD full screen, you can have your movie appear in a floating window, instead. That way you can do other things while the movie is playing in the background, like check your email, buy more DVDs, etc. To do that, just press the Esc key on your keyboard. When you're in this floating window mode, you'll see a separate floating DVD Player Controller Bar, which you'll use instead of the pop-up controller you use while in Full Screen mode.

MacTip: Watching Microsoft Windows Media Videos

If you want to watch Windows Media Video files (video designed to play in Microsoft's native video format for PCs, known as WMV files), you can download a free utility called Flip4Mac (www.microsoft.com/mac/products/flip4mac.mspx), which lets you watch these files seamlessly on your Mac. Highly recommended.

Chapter Eight

Managing Your Photos with iPhoto

How to Keep Track of, Organize, and Have Fun with Your Photos

Another big reason people buy computers today is so they can organize, print, and just plain see the photos from their digital cameras. Every computer out there comes with software that will let you do that to some extent, but only the Mac comes with iPhoto, and there's no other free application out there like it. In fact, iPhoto is so amazing that a lot of people buy Macs just to be able to use iPhoto—it's that great. Now, if that sounds like marketing hype, it's only because you haven't tried iPhoto, because once you do, you'll become a die-hard iPhoto evangelist who'll become annoying at a level that will make you intolerable to co-workers, friends, and even family members. Oh, at first, they'll be really impressed, because iPhoto lets you do some really amazing things with photos (like creating printed books, and printed calendars, and professional-looking greeting cards, and on and on), but there will come this point where you "cross over the line" and withdraw from normal society into a world only other iPhoto users can relate to. My buddy Terry White (one of this book's tech editors) has a great analogy for this type of thing, which he relates to Star Trek conventions. He says that going to Star Trek conventions is fine, and even planning your family vacation around traveling to a city where they're holding a Star Trek convention is still okay, but once you put on a Star Trek costume to attend the convention, you've crossed the line. So, be forewarned, this type of obsessive behavior is a possible side effect of using iPhoto. When people see the things you create in iPhoto, and start saying things like, "Wow, you did this?" and "This looks so professional," it can become very intoxicating, and before you know it, you're standing in line to get an autograph from Counselor Deanna Troi, and you're dressed as a Ferengi. Don't say I didn't warn you.

Getting Photos onto Your Mac, Step 1

Photos can come from a lot of places, and getting them from most of these places is really simple. Getting photos from your digital camera onto your Mac is pretty easy, but a little different, so we'll start with that. You could connect your digital camera directly to your computer, using the USB cable that came with your camera, and while that will work, it's so crazy slow (which makes the process take so long) that I couldn't recommend it to you with a straight face. Instead, you'll really need to get a memory card reader—just pop your memory card out of your digital camera and slide it into the card reader. Then plug the card reader into your Mac's USB slot and your memory card will appear right on your desktop, so you can access all your photos quickly. The good news is they're pretty inexpensive (for example, the SanDisk Extreme USB 2.0 Card Reader, which reads both CompactFlash and SD memory cards, has a street price of around $20). So, that's where we start. Get a card reader, and getting your photos onto your Mac will get faster and easier.

Getting Photos onto Your Mac, Step 2

Installed on every Mac since I can remember is an application called iPhoto, which we use to import and manage our photos (and it does a pretty brilliant job of it). When you plug in that memory card reader we just talked about, iPhoto will automatically launch so you can import your photos. (*Note*: If, for some reason, iPhoto doesn't automatically launch, just launch it yourself by clicking on the iPhoto icon in the Dock. If it's not in the Dock, look for it in your Applications folder. If for some weird reason you don't have iPhoto [hey, it's possible], then turn to Chapter 9 for what to do instead.) We'll assume that you have iPhoto, and when you plugged in your memory card, it launched (because that's almost certainly what will happen). Once iPhoto appears, you'll see iPhoto's import window, and thumbnails of all the photos on your memory card will appear in that window (as seen above). In the Event Name field at the bottom of the window, go ahead and type in a short name that describes what these photos are (for example, "Italy Vacation," or "Zak's Birthday," etc.), and then in the Description field below that, type in a full description of these photos (for example, "Our family vacation to Italy in June of 2008," or "Shots we took on that cruise"). If you want to import all the photos on that memory card, just click the Import All button. If you only want to import certain photos, first click on one of them, then press-and-hold the Command key (the key with the clover icon or Apple logo on it), and click on any other individual photos you want to select for importing. Now click on the Import Selected button to import just those photos.

Getting Photos onto Your Mac, Step 3

When you click either of those Import buttons in iPhoto, your photos are copied from your memory card onto your Mac. Once the importing is done, since you've copied the images onto your Mac, it asks if you want to delete those images or keep the originals on the memory card. The choice to delete or not delete is yours, but as a member in good standing of the paranoid photographers club, I don't erase photos off my memory card until I have them copied to two different places—like one copy on my Mac and one copy on a DVD—but that's just me. Now that your photos are on your Mac, and inside iPhoto, you can see them by clicking on Events in the Source list (under Library at the top left of the window), and then double-clicking on the event in the viewing area (each event is represented by a large thumbnail). Once you're looking inside an event, you can use the buttons along the bottom of the window to do different things with your photos—like order prints (online); email photos; create photo books, Web galleries, greeting cards, or calendars; or you can just print your photos out on your own printer.

Putting Your Favorite Photos One Click Away

When you double-click on an event in iPhoto, it shows you all the photos you imported when that event was created, but that might include all the photos from your memory card (if you clicked the Import All button), including the shots that, well…aren't so great (the out-of-focus shots, the ones where you accidentally took a shot of your foot, etc.). So, to give you one-click access to the best photos from that event (the "keepers"), you'd create an Album, and drag your best photos in there. To do this, just click the little + (plus sign) button in iPhoto's bottom-left corner. This tells iPhoto that you want to create something new, and you get to tell it exactly what that is from the dialog that pops down from the top of the window. In this case, you want to create an album, so you'd click on the Album icon (if it's not already selected), give it a name in the Name field, and then click the Create button. This adds a new empty album to the list under Albums on the left side of iPhoto (since your album is empty, you won't see anything in the viewing area). To add photos to your album, start by going back to Events and double-clicking on your event, so you can see the photos inside of it. Then, click-and-drag the photos you want in your new album onto that album in the Source list. Now, anytime you want to see those "keepers" you can just click on that album.

Sorting Your Photos in iPhoto

Once your photos are in an album in iPhoto (see previous page), you can rearrange their order by simply dragging-and-dropping them into the order you'd like them to appear. This is particularly important if you're going to be building a slide show, and you want to choose which photo appears first, second, etc. However, you can also have iPhoto automatically sort your photos by date, keyword, title (alphabetically by name), or by rating (where you can assign a 1- to 5-star rating to the photos in your album by pressing Command-1 for a 1-star rating, Command-2 for a 2-star rating, etc.). You can choose these automatic sorting options by going under the View menu, under Sort Photos (you'll see a list of your choices right there).

Cropping Photos

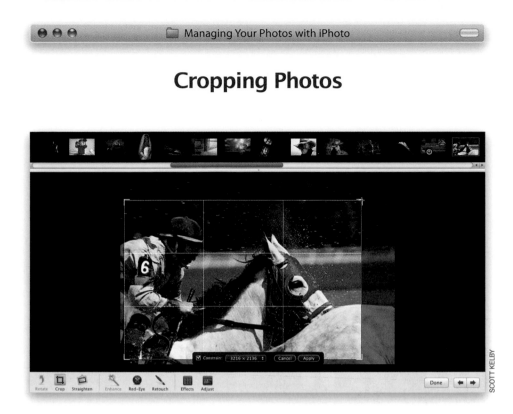

SCOTT KELBY

When it comes to editing your photos, iPhoto gives you a surprising amount of options, and since one of the things people do most to photos is crop them, here's how it's done: First, click on the photo you want to edit, then click the Edit button beneath the viewing area in the bottom-left corner (its icon is a pencil). This brings you to the editing window, and a list of tools appears beneath the viewing area. Here you'll want to click on the Crop button. This brings up a cropping border around your photo, and everything that appears inside that border will remain visible. So, to crop your photo, first turn on the Constrain checkbox (so your photo's aspect ratio will stay the same), then click to grab either side of the border, the top, the bottom, or one of the corners (as shown here), and drag inward. You can readjust the position of the cropping border by clicking-and-dragging inside the border (your cursor will change into a hand cursor), and you can drag the border around your photo to position it right where you want it. When it's sized and positioned the way you'd like it, click the Apply button at the bottom right of the image, then click the Done button near the bottom-right corner of the window.

Removing Red Eye

KATHY SILER AND SCOTT KELBY

If your photo has the dreaded red eye, it's easy enough to fix. First, click on the photo where your subject has red eye, then click the Edit button beneath the viewing area of the iPhoto window. Now just click on the Red Eye button (found beneath the viewing area), then simply click on your subject's eyes and the red eye is gone. See, I told you it was easy enough to fix. When you're done editing your photo, click the Done button near the bottom-right corner of the window.

> **X MacTip: Color Correcting Your Photos in iPhoto**
>
> If you have a color problem in your photo, chances are it's because the white balance wasn't set properly in your digital camera (Auto white balance is sometimes easy to fool), but you can fix it quickly if you know this trick: First, click on the Edit button at the bottom of iPhoto's window, then when the Edit toolbar appears across the bottom, click on the Adjust button to bring up the floating Adjust palette. To the left of the Tint slider is a little eyedropper tool. This tool sets your white balance, but don't click it on something white in your photo—instead click it on something in your photo that's supposed to be light gray, and it will adjust your color for the lighting situation it was shot in, and that will most likely fix most of your color problems.

Fixing Your Color, Brightness, and More

If the quality of your photo needs some adjusting, you can fix a number of the most common problems you're likely to run into using iPhoto's Adjust palette. So, go ahead and click on the photo you want to fix, click on the Edit button (the one with a pencil), and then click on the Adjust button beneath the viewing area. When the palette appears, you can adjust everything from the overall brightness of your photo (the Exposure slider) to the white balance (the Temperature and Tint sliders). Now, I've led you this far (to the Adjust palette), but I'm going to let iPhoto take it from here, because as you move your cursor over any of the sliders in the palette, a little description of what each slider does appears right over the slider. I do want to point out two things, though: (1) You can adjust to your heart's content, and when you're done, you can just close the palette (click on the little X in the upper-left corner). You can reopen this Adjust palette any time and tweak the photo some more, or if you want to return the photo to how it looked when you first started, just click on the Reset button in the bottom-left corner of the palette. (2) There are Copy and Paste buttons in the bottom right of the palette. This is cooler than it sounds. Let's say you open a photo and you tweak it so it's just the way you like it. If you have other similar photos that could use that same adjustment, click on the Copy button and then close the palette. Open another similar photo, click on the Edit and Adjust buttons, and then just click on the Paste button, and those settings you had copied from the previous photo will be applied to this photo. A huge time saver.

One–Click Special Effects (Like Black & White)

SCOTT KELBY

If you think your photo might look better in black and white (or in sepia tone, or with darkened edges), you can apply these looks with just a few clicks. Start by selecting a photo, then click the Edit button (the one with the pencil) beneath the viewing area of iPhoto's window. Then click the Effects button that appears beneath the viewing area to bring up the one-click Effects palette. The palette shows your original photo in the center, surrounded by eight versions of your photo, each with a different effect applied to it. To apply one of these effects, you just click on it. But the cool thing is, you also get to choose the intensity of the effect (except for B&W and Sepia). Once you click on an effect, a little number will appear between two arrows at the bottom of that effect in the palette. Keep clicking on the effect to make it more intense, or click on the left arrow to make it less intense (if you click back past 1, it removes the effect, or you can simply click on the center Original photo). After you've applied one effect, you can apply more effects on top of that by just clicking on them one by one. When you're done applying effects, close the palette by clicking the little X in the upper-left corner. When you're done editing your photo altogether, click the Done button near the bottom-right corner of the window.

Creating Slide Shows in iPhoto

In iPhoto, you can create pro-quality slide shows with nice, smooth transitions between photos (or blends, or even movement if you'd like). You have lots of control with them, it's easy to share the slide show you've created, and you can even add music. Best of all, creating slide shows in iPhoto is simple. Here's how it's done: First, click on the album of photos you want in your slide show, then click the + (plus sign) button in the bottom-left corner of iPhoto. When the dialog pops down from the top of the iPhoto window, click on the Slideshow icon, give your slide show a name, and then click the Create button. This adds a new slide show to the list of slide shows in the Source list on the left side of the iPhoto window (your new slide show's name may be highlighted. You can change the name of it, if you want, or just press the Return key to keep it), and a list of slide show controls appears at the bottom of the viewing area. Click on the Settings button, and a dialog with a list of options for your slide show pops down from the top of the window. This is where you choose (from top to bottom), how long each slide will stay onscreen, how fast the transition between slides will be, and a host of other options (including adding movement using the Ken Burns effect). Once you've made your choices, click the OK button, and then to watch your slide show, click on the Play button on the lower-left side of the viewing area.

Adding Music to Your iPhoto Slide Show

SCOTT KELBY

A silent slide show is a boring slide show, and nothing adds impact and emotion to a slide show of your photography like adding background music. Luckily, adding music to your slide show is easy and, by default, iPhoto has this feature turned on when you create your slide show. So, first click on your slide show in the Source list on the left side of the iPhoto window. Then click on the Music button at the bottom of the viewing area (it looks like the iTunes icon) and a dialog pops down from the top of the window. iPhoto comes with some free sample songs you can use in your slide shows, and you'll find them in the Sample Music folder at the top of the dialog (the first song in this folder is the default song you'll hear when you first create and play your slide show). To hear a preview of one of the songs in the list, click on the song and then click on the Play button at the bottom left of the dialog. To stop the preview, click on the Play button again. There's a search field to the right of the Play button that lets you search for songs from your choices in the dialog. For instance, if you want to search your entire iTunes Music library, click on Music under iTunes, then when you search, it searches your whole Music library. When you find the song you want, just click on it (of course, you can click on the Play button to hear a preview first to make sure it's the right song, or the right version of the song), then click the OK button. Now, when you click the Play button to see your slide show, the background music you chose will play.

Emailing Your Slide Show to Other People

SCOTT KELBY

If you want to send your finished slide show to somebody, it's easy—you just have to decide whether you want to burn your slide show to a DVD and send that out, or save the slide show as a QuickTime movie, so you can either email it or post it on the Web. Here, we'll make a movie (on the next page, we'll burn a DVD); first, click on the slide show (in the list of slide shows in the Source list on the left side of the iPhoto window), then go under the File menu and choose Export. A dialog (that you see above) is going to pop down from the top of iPhoto's window, and this is where you choose how big your movie is going to be from the Movie Size pop-up menu. If you're going to email the slide show, I would recommend choosing Medium (320x240) (as shown above), so it doesn't get too large to email (many people have a 5-MB limit on the size of an email they can accept, so smaller is usually better). Name your movie and choose where you want to save it, then click Export. It takes just a minute or two for the slide show to export as a movie, and it automatically embeds the music you used. (*Note*: If the music you're using for your slide show is rights-protected music purchased from the iTunes Store, the music will only play on computers you've authorized to play purchased music, so you might be better off using music you've imported from a CD, which doesn't have that limitation.) Once your slide show is done, you can just drag-and-drop it into an email message.

Putting Your iPhoto Slide Show on a DVD

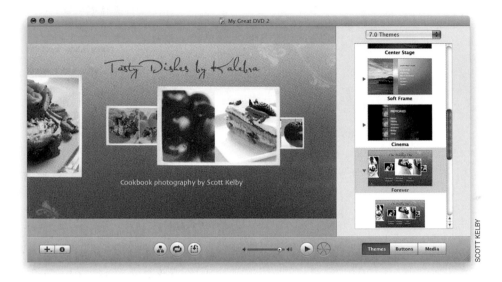

If you want to put your slide show on a DVD (so the person you're sending it to can watch it on their TV or computer), in the Source list, click on the slide show you want on DVD. Go under the Share menu, choose Send to iDVD (iDVD is Apple's application for creating DVDs, and comes free with all Macs), and then click the Send Whole Slideshow button in the resulting iDVD Export dialog. It will then prepare the photos, launch iDVD, and open your slide show in the iDVD window. Here, you can choose a theme for the main menu you see when you put a traditional movie DVD into a DVD player. Since we're just making a quick DVD slide show, I recommend just scrolling through the list of themes on the right side of the iDVD window, and finding a theme best suited for your slide show. Then go under iDVD's Project menu and choose Autofill Drop Zones. This automatically adds photos from your slide show into your theme, so now the theme is customized with your look, as seen above (you can manually choose images, too, but for now we're doing this the quick and easy way). You can change any text by clicking on it once to move it, or double-clicking on it to edit it or change the font or size. To see a preview of the animated opening main screen, click the Preview DVD Playback button at the bottom right of the preview area. To return to the themes screen, click the Stop button in the little floating iDVD Remote Control that appears to the right of the window. When you're finished customizing the look, insert a blank DVD into your DVD burner and click the Burn button (it's just to the right of the Preview DVD Playback button). (*Note:* Your Mac must have a SuperDrive or be connected to an external DVD burning drive to burn DVDs.)

Emailing Photos (from iPhoto)

If you have some photos in iPhoto that you want to email to someone, just select them (click on one photo, press-and-hold the Command key, then click on the other photos), then click the Email button at the bottom of the iPhoto window. This will bring up a dialog asking how large you want the images in your email to be. If you're emailing a lot of photos, you might want to choose a smaller size for your photos, so your email doesn't get bounced back to you because the person you're emailing has a size limit on the emails they receive (a 5-MB limit per email is pretty common). Once you've made your size choice, you can also choose whether you want the file's name included, or any comments you've added (captions), then click the Compose button, and it will launch Mail (Apple's email application), insert your photos into a mail message, and if you left the checkboxes turned on for including your titles and comments, they will appear right below each photo. Pretty slick. Now, you might be wondering how to get those comments into your photos? It's easy. Just click on the photo you want to add a caption to, and then click on the little Information button (the "i" button in the bottom-left corner of iPhoto's window). A little panel will pop-up from right above it with info about the photo itself (when it was taken, which file format it is, etc.), and you'll see a Description field at the bottom. Click once on that field to highlight it, type in your caption, and then click the "i" button again to close it. That's it—you've added a caption that can now appear below your emailed photo automatically, each time you email it.

Putting Your Photos on the Web Using .Mac

Would you like to publish "The American Landscape (Photography by Scott Kelby)" to your Web Gallery?

This will create an album in scottkelby's Web Gallery on .Mac. The album can be viewed with Safari or any modern web browser. The title of this album will be visible to everyone viewing your Web Gallery.

Album Viewable by: Everyone

Allow: ☐ Downloading of photos or entire album
☐ Uploading of photos via web browser
☑ Adding of photos via email

Show: ☑ Photo titles
☐ Email address for uploading photos

Show Advanced   Cancel   Publish

Edit Rotate Hide Flag   Book Calendar Card   Web Gallery Email Print Order Prints iWeb

SCOTT KELBY

If you have a .Mac account, you can not only have iPhoto create an instant online photo gallery for you, you can add photos to your online gallery by simply emailing them. Here's how: First, click on the album you want to post online as an online gallery. Then go under the Share menu, choose Web Gallery, and the dialog you see above pops down from the top of the iPhoto window. First, choose who you want to be able to see this online gallery from the pop-up menu (everyone, just people you give a password to, or just you), then under that, you can choose if you want to let people who visit your gallery have the ability to download your photos. You can also choose if you want to be able to upload photos from any Web browser, or if it can just be updated with new photos via email. Lastly, you can choose if you want the names of your files posted below the images, and if you want to post a visible email address where people who you've let see your gallery can add their own images. On the next page, we'll look at what happens once you click the Publish button.

Finding Your Online Gallery

SCOTT KELBY

When you click the Publish button, it uploads your photos and adds a new online gallery section in the Source list on the left side of the iPhoto window, under the header Web Gallery. When it's done uploading, look up in the upper-left corner of the iPhoto viewing area; you'll see the Web address where your new Web gallery is found (as seen above). If you click on that Web address, it launches your Web browser and takes you to your new gallery. You can delete Web galleries from right within iPhoto: you just click on the Web gallery (in the Source list), and then press the Delete key on your keyboard. A little warning dialog pops down to let you know that you're not just deleting this album in iPhoto, it's also going to stop publishing your online gallery, and since that's what we want (in this case, anyway), you'd click the Delete button.

Choosing the Look of Your Online Gallery

Once you visit your online gallery, you can choose the look you want for it. There are four different layouts to choose from—Grid, Mosaic (shown above), Carousel (which looks like a Finder window's Cover Flow view), and Slideshow—and you can choose these in the bottom-left corner of the Web Gallery window. On the lower-right side of the window, you can choose the background color behind your gallery by clicking on the Color radio buttons, and you can also choose the size of your thumbnails by using the slider. You also have the choice of leaving a set of options visible at the top of your gallery for people who view it, or you can hide them from view by clicking the Hide Options button in the upper-right corner.

Updating Your Online Web Gallery

You add photos to your online Web gallery right within iPhoto—just drag-and-drop photos you want added onto your Web gallery's album on the left side of the iPhoto window (make sure it's the album that appears in the Web Gallery section). Then, once you've dragged over all the photos you want added to your gallery, it uploads them and updates your Web gallery online (if it does not automatically update, click once on the little radar-looking icon that appears to the right of your Web gallery's name [as shown here], and then refresh [reload] the page in your Web browser). If you turned on the checkboxes to update the gallery using email and to show the email address, you'll see the email address you'll need to email (with your photos attached to the email), in the upper-right corner of iPhoto's viewing area. You can also add photos to your Web gallery from your Web browser (well, as long as you chose that option before you hit the Publish button). Just go to the webpage, and up in the options that appear across the top, click on the Upload button. This pops down a dialog asking you to enter your name, email address (or URL), and a set of image characters. Then choose which file you want to upload by clicking on the Choose Files button. Click back on your Web gallery and it uploads. To delete a photo from your Web gallery, in iPhoto, click on the Web gallery album, and then click on the photo you want to delete. Press the Delete key on your keyboard and that removes it from your iPhoto Web gallery album, but it won't remove it from your online Web gallery until you click the little radar icon to the right of the gallery's name. Refresh the webpage and it will update with your change.

How to Hide an Online Gallery

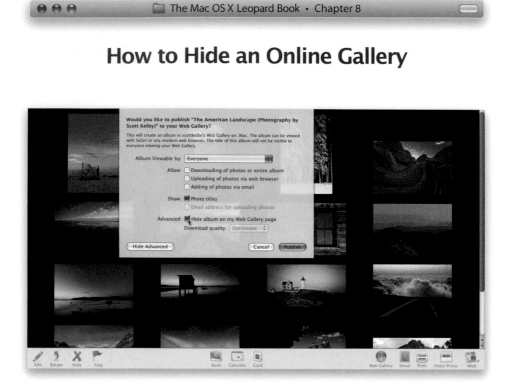

If you have published a Web gallery that you don't want everyone to see when they visit your main gallery page, you can hide it from view by choosing that option before you hit the Publish button—but you have to know where that option is (it's sort of hidden). When you create your Web gallery by clicking on your album in iPhoto, and then going under the Share menu and choosing Web Gallery, a dialog pops down from the top of the iPhoto window. Click on the Show Advanced button in the bottom-left corner and the dialog will expand, revealing an option to hide the album. Just turn on the Hide Album on My Web Gallery Page checkbox, and the album will be hidden on your main gallery page.

Making Photo Books: Choosing Your Theme

SCOTT KELBY

One of the coolest things you can do with iPhoto is create your own custom, printed photo book (it sounds hard, but it couldn't be easier—you design it in iPhoto using one of the built-in templates as a starting place, then you click one button to upload the photos to the lab, and they print, bind, and ship the book directly to you in just a few days). Every time I show an Apple photo book to someone, they're always amazed at how cool they are, and at this point, I make a photo book after every vacation or special event with my family. To make a book, start by creating a new album in iPhoto with the photos you want to appear in the printed book (see page 169), then click the Book button at the bottom of the iPhoto window. A dialog will pop down from the top (seen above) where you make two decisions: (1) how large to make your printed book and whether you want it to be hardcover or softcover (from the Book Type pop-up menu at the top), and (2) which theme to base your book upon (there are different ones to choose from—from travel to formal wedding books, from family albums to fine art layouts). Professionals design the layouts for these books and they make ideal starting places for you to create your own custom look by adding your own photos and text (which we'll look at on the next page). For now, pick your book type and click the Choose button, which takes you to where you can start building your book.

Making Photo Books: Arranging Your Photos

SCOTT KELBY

Once you've chosen your type and theme, it's time to drag-and-drop your photos into the layout. If this is your first time building a photo book, I recommend clicking the Autoflow button at the bottom of the window (as shown here). This takes all the photos in your album and automatically places them throughout the book for you. Now, of course, iPhoto has no idea which photo you want where, so it places them in there randomly (but don't worry—after they're in place, you can move them around yourself and put them right where you want them). So, first click on Autoflow, and then scroll through your book and see how things look (I'm often surprised to find out that some of the photos it has put together on the same page actually look pretty good). If you want to make a change, you can literally drag-and-drop photos within pages (when you drag one photo and drop it on another, they swap places). If you want to move a photo to a completely different page, just drag it from the current page in the viewing area, and drop it onto the page you want it be on up in the filmstrip across the top. If you want to change the number of photos on a particular page, go up to the filmstrip, click on the page you want to edit, then click-and-hold on the Layout button at the bottom of the window and a menu will pop up with your choices for how many photos can fit on that page.

Making Photo Books: Customizing Backgrounds

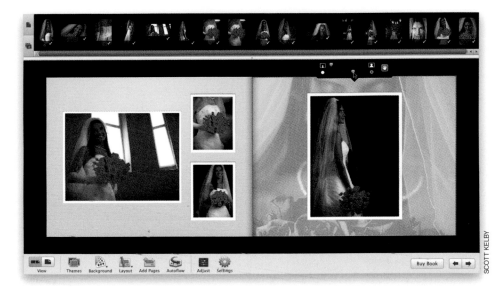

SCOTT KELBY

Besides choosing which photo goes where (and how many photos appear on each page), you can choose the background color behind your photos, however the number of background style choices will depend on which theme you chose. For example, if you chose the Picture Book theme, your background choices will be white, gray, black, or you can use any photo in your album as your background. However, if you chose a Travel theme, your background choices are only beige, dark brown with stripes, or to have a photo as your background. You choose your background by clicking on the Background button at the bottom of the window and making your choice from the pop-up menu. If you choose to make a photo your background, you then have to choose a photo and drag-and-drop it onto that background. (*Note*: To switch from viewing pages in the filmstrip to viewing your photos, just click on the View buttons on the left side of the filmstrip.) If you click on a background photo once it's in place, two sliders appear: the top slider adjusts the size of the background photo; the bottom slider allows you to lighten the photo so it doesn't distract from the main photo on the page (as shown here).

X MacTip: Manually Building Photo Books

If you'd rather place each photo into your photo book individually (rather than using the Autoflow feature), it's easy. You'll see that all the photos in your album appear in the filmstrip up top, and you can just drag-and-drop the photos where you want them to appear in your layout.

Making Photo Books: Changing Layouts

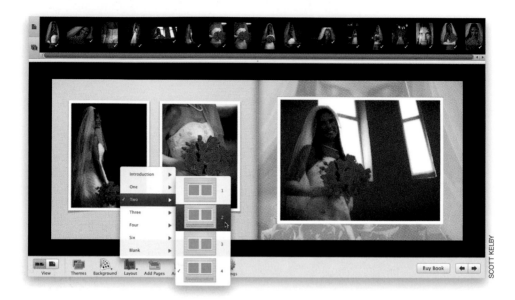

Not only do you get to choose how many photos go on a page, you usually get the choice of how these photos actually appear on the page (it just depends on the theme, but usually you get a choice). For example, in the Contemporary theme, for a one-photo page, you get four layout choices—your one photo fills the entire page; it appears in the top center of the page, but large; it appears centered, but smaller; or it appears as a long, wide image across the page, edge-to-edge (with lots of white space above and below it, like a panoramic image). You choose these by clicking-and-holding on the Layout button at the bottom of the window. A pop-up menu will appear with the choices for the number of images on the page, each with a submenu with little thumbnails that show what your page layout will look like (as shown here in the Formal theme). You can customize each page in the book using this method, so it really gets that "custom-designed by you" look. Once all your pages look the way you want, they're in the order you want (up in the filmstrip, you can drag-and-drop pages or spreads into the order you want), and you've entered in your captions, cover text, and intro page text (by just clicking on the default text that's there and entering your own), you're set to go—just click the Buy Book button (at the bottom right of the window) and place your order (you'll see your prices, shipping options, etc., just like when you buy anything online). It will automatically upload your photos to Apple, and they take it from there. *Warning*: Once you print one photo book, and see how slick they come out, you'll be ordering these books again, and again, and again.

Making Photo Greeting Cards

The same way you can have professional-looking photo books printed and delivered to you, you can also create custom-made, lab-printed cards, as well. There are a number of different styles to choose from, and depending on which style you choose, the cover can either have one or more photos. So, click on a photo, then click on the Card button beneath the viewing area of the iPhoto window. A dialog will pop down from the top of the window with a selection of different cards for different occasions. Once you find the card you want, you'll see how many photos it accommodates, and once you've determined that, click the Cancel button. So, let's say that, like in the example shown above, your card can have four photos total (three on the cover and one on the inside). Go to an album and Command-click on the four photos you want to use, then click on the Card button. Find that card template again and then click the Choose button. This puts your selected photos into the card. You can enlarge and adjust the position of each photo in the card by clicking once on a photo and a little editing bar will appear above it. Use the slider to change the size, and click on the Hand tool to click-and-drag your image inside the window to adjust its position. You can also click on the default text to customize the text. When you're done, click on the Buy Card button, and choose how many you want, where you want them sent, etc.

Creating Photo Calendars

I've given iPhoto calendars as a gift and I can say from personal experience, they are a huge hit (it makes a perfect Mother's Day or holiday gift). Start by going to an album and selecting the photos you'd like to appear on your custom calendar, then click the Calendar button beneath the viewing area of the iPhoto window. A dialog will pop down from the top of the window and this is where you choose which style you'd like for your calendar (they're similar in design to the iPhoto book themes). Click on your style and then click Choose. This pops down another dialog where you decide: (a) the month your calendar starts and how many months your calendar will include, (b) whether your calendar will include your country's national holidays (from the Show National Holidays pop-up menu), and (c) if you want events from your Apple iCal calendar automatically imprinted on your calendar. There's also a checkbox you can turn on to have iPhoto automatically add any birthdays you have added to contacts in your ress Book (as shown here). Not too shabby, eh? When you're done with these es, click the OK button. When the Calendar page loads, you can click-and-drag os onto your calendar one by one or click the Autoflow button to have it automati-ill your calendar with your photos. Like the photo books, you can click on the ut button beneath the viewing area to add more than one photo to a calendar (if you need more photos to fill your calendar, just go back to your albums and and-drop photos onto your calendar in the Source list). In fact, it pretty much like a photo book (as far as building it goes), except for the fact that it doesn't let hange the background color.

Sending Out for Prints

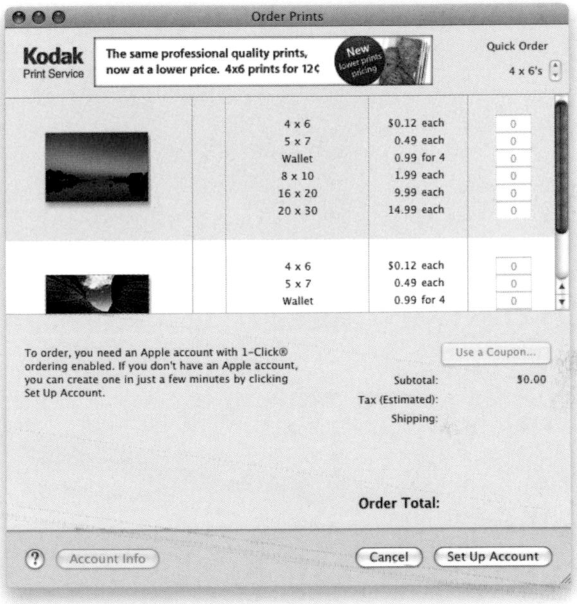

If you don't have your own photo-quality printer, you can send out your photos and have professional-quality color prints made, just like you'd get from your local CVS or Walgreens, but it's more convenient because you just select the photos you want as prints, then click the Order Prints button near the bottom-right corner of the iPhoto window. This connects you directly to Kodak's online lab, and brings up the Kodak Order Prints window (shown above). Here, you choose the size you want for your prints (from the standard 4x6" prints up to 20x30" poster-sized prints), and how many you want of each print. Just enter your choices, and click the Set Up Account button. Set up an Apple account, if you don't already have one, and enter your billing information. Once you submit your order, your photos are sent from iPhoto to Kodak, and then once printed, they're sent directly to you.

Printing Your Own Photos

If you have your own photo-quality printer, you can make your own prints directly from iPhoto. First, select the photos you want to print, and then click the Print button in the bottom right of iPhoto's window. The printing dialog you see above will pop down. There are five different printing layouts to choose from, including a contact sheet that lets you print multiple photos on one single sheet. This dialog is also where you choose which printer you'll be printing to, the size paper you'll be printing on, and the quality. Once it's all selected, hit the Print button, sit back, and wait for your prints to come rolling out.

X MacTip: Sending Large Photos Without Getting Bounced Back

Many people have a limit on the size email they can receive (a 5-MB limit is pretty common), and if you try to send someone a number of photos, your email might be rejected (bounced back) by your friend's email provider. A way around this is to iChat with them instead, and then once you're chatting, drag-and-drop the photos you want to send into the message area of the iChat window, and they'll be delivered to the person you're iChatting with, without any fear of bounceback. When sending multiple files, you'll have to compress them into a single archive first.

More Tips for Using iPhoto on Your Mac

X MacTip: Rate Your Photos in Full-Screen Mode

It's much easier to assign 1- to 5-star ratings to your photos if you can see them large enough to make a decent decision. You can do that by clicking on the album you just imported, then clicking the Play Slideshow button at the bottom left of the iPhoto window to take you into Full Screen mode. This brings up a Slideshow dialog, where I recommend turning on the checkbox for Show My Ratings. Now, as the photos play, you can press 1–5 on your keyboard to assign ratings to your photos. To remove a rating, press 0 (zero).

X MacTip: Quickly Assign Ratings to More Than One Photo at a Time

If you want to assign a similar rating to a number of photos (like all your 5-star photos), you can press-and-hold the Command key, click on all the photos you want to be 5-star rated, then just press 5 (while still holding the Command key), and all the selected photos are assigned that rating.

X MacTip: Undoing Your iPhoto Edits

If you've edited a photo in iPhoto (for example, if you've color corrected a photo, cropped it, sharpened it, etc.), you can undo those changes with just one click—just Control-click (or Right-click) on the photo, then from the contextual menu, choose Revert to Original.

X MacTip: Shortcut for Importing Photos into iPhoto

If you have a bunch of photos you want imported into iPhoto (either from a folder or from a memory card), just select the photos (Command-click on each of them), and then drag-and-drop them onto the iPhoto icon in the Dock, and they'll be imported into iPhoto.

X MacTip: Editing Photos in Another Image Editing Application

If you want to edit a photo on your Mac using something other than iPhoto, choose an external editor from iPhoto's General preferences, then just Control-click (or Right-click) on the photo's icon. From the contextual menu, choose Edit in External Editor and the photo will open in the application you chose (for example, if you have Adobe Photoshop and want to edit the photo there). You can also Control-click on the photo's icon in a Finder window and choose Open With, then choose the application.

Chapter Nine

Working with Photos on Your Mac

How to Make Your Still Images Come to Life

These days, about every computer out there lets you import and look at digital photos, but your Mac takes photography to a whole new level because it doesn't let you just look at photos—it lets you use your photos in really creative ways. To uncork this photography genie, start by using iPhoto (as I showed you in the previous chapter). It's a brilliantly designed application that is kind of the hub for photos on your Mac, and once your photos are in there, you can access them (and do creative things with them) from a bunch of other applications, and because of that, you'll use photography more than people using other computers. Now, not only does your Mac manage your photos, it takes 'em. If you've got a MacBook, MacBook Pro, MacBook Air, or iMac, you've got a built-in camera that can take photos of you at times when you really shouldn't have a photo taken. You see, most folks are relatively concerned about their appearance, and when they know that a photo is about to be taken, they generally try to look their very best. However, since Apple introduced Photo Booth (which is a clever take-off on the photo booths you see in the mall), people routinely do things to photos of themselves you wouldn't wish on an enemy. So, unless you have a high tolerance for personal anguish, I'd stay away from Photo Booth, because although it will create a normal photo of you, you know, and I know, that you're going to click on the Effects button, and then you're going to not only do horrible things to your self-portrait, but because there's an Email button right there, you're going to send this to someone else, and you'll have a lot of laughs about it, too, until it ends up on their MySpace page....

Downloading Photos from the Web

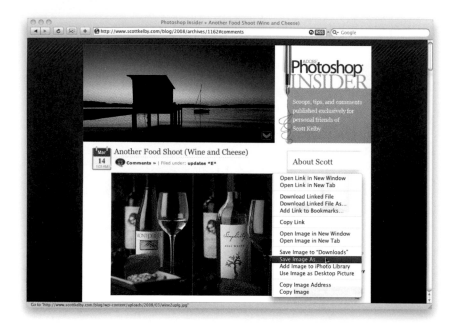

If you're using the Safari Web browser and you see a photo you'd like to keep, in most cases you can download that photo to your Mac by pressing-and-holding the Control key and clicking on the photo, which brings up a contextual menu. (*Note*: If you have a two-button mouse, you can just Right-click on the photo, if you have your mouse set up this way.) You've got a few choices here: If you want to import this photo right into iPhoto, choose Add Image to iPhoto Library. If you just want to save this photo to your desktop, choose Save Image As, and then choose where you want to save it (your desktop, in this case), or if you just want to copy this photo into your Mac's memory (so you can copy-and-paste the photo into an email, or a text document, etc.), then choose Copy Image. Now you can paste that photo by just Control-clicking where you want it, and selecting Paste from the contextual menu.

Importing Photos Without iPhoto

```
●  ●  ○                Lexar RW–019

         Download To:  ▢ Pictures, Movies, and Music folders ▼

      Automatic Task:  None                                  ▼

                       Occurs after downloading

         Items to download:  83


   ( Options... )         ( Download Some... )  ( Download All )
```

If you want to import photos from your digital camera, and for some reason you don't have iPhoto on your Mac (maybe you bought a used Mac, and the person who owned it before you uninstalled it), here are two other easy ways to import photos: (1) Insert your memory card into a card reader (or attach your camera to your Mac with a USB cable) and launch Image Capture (it's in your Applications folder), which lets you import photos into a folder you choose on your Mac (by default, it chooses your Pictures folder). The Import dialog is similar to iPhoto's—it lets you import all the photos on the memory card or just selected ones. Also, once you're done importing, you can choose to have an Automatic Task applied to your imported photos. This lets you choose what you want to do next, after import, including having your photos automatically cropped to a certain size, or fitted into certain common dimensions (like a 5x7", 8x10", etc.). You can have them opened in Apple's Preview application (more on Preview in a few pages), or you can just have them imported and do nothing (choose None from the Automatic Task pop-up menu). If you click the Options button, it brings up a dialog with preferences, including the option of deleting your images off the memory card once they're imported. The second way to import photos (2) is to simply access your memory card (with a card reader or USB cable) and when it appears on your desktop (just like your hard drive appears there), you can just drag-and-drop the photos from your memory card into a folder on your Mac.

Viewing Photos Using Quick Look

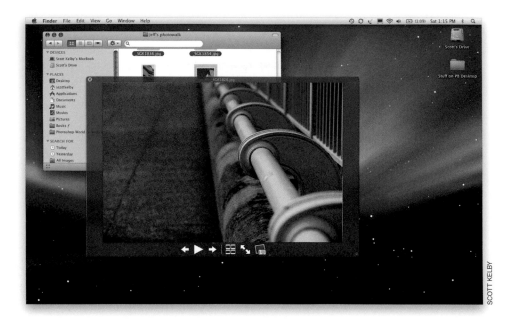

SCOTT KELBY

If you have a photo you'd like to take a quick look at, use Quick Look. Just click on the photo (on your desktop or in a Finder window) and then press the Spacebar. This instantly opens your photo onscreen in its own separate window. If you'd like to see that photo in a full-screen view, click the diagonal arrows at the bottom center of the window. If you'd like to add this photo to your iPhoto library, click the little iPhoto camera icon at the bottom of the window. You can also open multiple photos at once in Quick Look— just Command-click on all the photos you want to view, then press the Spacebar. This adds Previous and Next arrows to the bottom of the Quick Look window, so you can move through your photos. There's also a button (which looks like two rows of slides), that takes you to a window with thumbnails of all your selected images in Quick Look, and you can click on any one to jump to that photo. To close Quick Look, press the little X in the top-left corner or just press the Spacebar again.

X MacTip: Using Quick Look in Mail

f somebody emails you a photo, you can view that photo in Quick Look just like you
ould a photo on your desktop or in a folder. Plus, you have all the same features,
luding the ability to view it full screen, or save the photo to your iPhoto library.
se Quick Look within Mail, just click the gray Quick Look button that appears
below your email address in the email you received.

Seeing an Instant Slide Show

SCOTT KELBY

Anytime you want to see an instant slide show of some images, just select them (Command-click on them on your desktop or in a Finder window), and then press the Spacebar to open them in Quick Look. You'll see a Play button at the bottom of the window, just click on it and you get an instant slide show. To see your slide show full screen, once it starts, click the Full Screen button (the diagonal arrows) to the right of the Play button. To stop the slide show, click the Pause button or press Command-W to close the Quick Look window. Easy enough.

X **MacTip: Moving Your Slide Show Controls in Quick Look**

If you're using Quick Look to view photos in Full Screen mode, you can move the slide show controls to anywhere you'd like onscreen by clicking-and-holding along the edge of the slide show controls box, then dragging-and-dropping it wherever you'd like.

Should You Use Preview to View Photos?

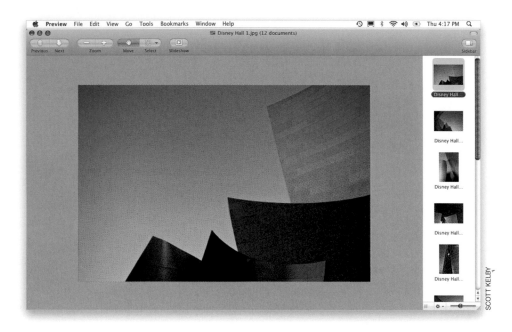

Apple includes a program called Preview on every Mac, which lets you open just about any type of image so you can view it, and it also has some image-editing features. Okay, so here's my problem with it: there's nothing wrong with Preview, but since Quick Look came along, I can't find any real reason to use Preview. If I want to do image editing (cropping, color correction, etc.), iPhoto is much more powerful, and if I just want to look at a photo, Quick Look is the quickest. So, my advice is, use Quick Look instead.

X MacTip: Getting Photos onto Your iPhone or iPod

The easiest way to get photos from your Mac onto your iPhone or iPod is to get them into iPhoto first—because iTunes lets you access, and upload, images from iPhoto right into your iPhone or iPod. When you plug your iPhone or iPod into your Mac, and iTunes launches, in the iPod preferences, you'll see a tab called Photos across the top. Click on that tab and you can choose which albums from iPhoto get transferred to your iPhone or iPod. Once you make your choices (by turning on the checkboxes beside the ones you want copied over after you chose Selected Albums), click the Apply button in the bottom-right corner and the photos are copied onto your iPhone or iPod.

Create Your Own Photos Using Photo Booth

If you bought an iMac, MacBook, MacBook Pro, or MacBook Air, they all come with a built-in camera, and they also all come with a very slick little program called Photo Booth, which lets you use that little built-in camera to take photos of you or your friends (or basically, anyone that sits in front of your computer). It's found in the Applications folder, and when you launch it, a window appears showing you what your Mac's camera is seeing. To take a photo, just click that round red camera button in the center beneath the image window. It beeps and gives you a 3-2-1 countdown, then your whole screen flashes to let you know it's taking your photo (this photo appears in the little filmstrip across the bottom of the Photo Booth window). If you click on your photo in the filmstrip, it displays the photo in the image window with a row of buttons beneath it that let you (left to right) email the photo to someone, add the photo to iPhoto, take another photo, add this photo as your login account photo, or use the photo as your Buddy Picture icon when you're using iChat for online chatting. To delete a photo from your filmstrip, just click on it and press the Delete key. But perhaps the coolest thing you can do with Photo Booth is to apply effects (see the next page for that).

201

Adding Effects to Your Photo Booth Photos

Effects are applied to your photo as the photo is taken, so to get back to that screen, click the round gray camera button just below your image window. Now, click the Effects button on the right and it takes you to an Effects preview window, which shows you what the camera is seeing (your normal photo is shown in the center) with eight different effects applied to your photo, including a sepia-tone effect, black-and-white effect, a pop-art look, and a number of others (as seen above). But there are more than just those eight; click the right arrow button (just to the right of the Effects button) and it takes you to another window of effects, which are more like funhouse mirror effects (and just in case you were wondering, no, I'm not going to show that here. That is to be only used in the privacy and sanctity of my home, where my children can see it and laugh at me hysterically. Sadly, I'm used to it).

Different Backgrounds in Photo Booth

SCOTT KELBY

Photo Booth has a very cool little feature that lets you put a fake background behind your image, in kind of the same way television meteorologists have a large map appear behind them—it's done using the green screen window of effects (click on the Effects button beneath the image window and then click the right arrow button twice). When you get to this effect window, you'll see a number of photos and video clips that Apple has already provided for you to use as backgrounds. Just click on the one you want to use and it may ask you to "Please step out of the frame" (so, just move to the left or right far enough, so you're no longer seen on-camera). Once Photo Booth detects the current background, it replaces it with the one you chose. Once you see it, you can step back in front of the camera, and voilá—you're on a new background. Now, just click the round red camera button to take your photo on this background.

X MacTip: Better Background Swapping

Although Photo Booth is creating a high-end-TV-and-Hollywood effect, it's not a high-end-TV-and-Hollywood green screen application, and the results you get are pretty much based on what kind of background you're standing in front of when you try this out. If you're against a plain background, it does a surprisingly good job. If you're on a real busy background, it has a harder time figuring out where the background ends and you start. So, for the best results, put as plain a background behind you as you can.

Use Your Own Backgrounds Instead

If you don't want to use Apple's built-in Photo Booth backgrounds (or you've used them so much that you're sick of them), you can add your own photos or videos. Just click on the Effects button, and then press the right arrow button (to the right of the Effects button) until you get over to the fourth set of effects. Now all you have to do is drag-and-drop a photo or video clip right onto any one of the eight open slots, and that background is now available to use as a green screen background behind photos of you.

Viewing Your Photos Using Front Row

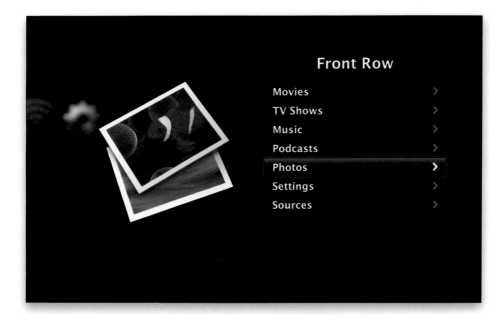

Your Mac is more than just a Mac—it's a very cool media center, where you can watch movies and downloaded TV shows, look at slide shows, listen to music, and all the cool stuff you want to do with your media, and you see it all full screen in its own separate application called Front Row. Even cooler, you can run it all with that little white remote that came with your Mac (ahhhh, so that's what that's for!). To enter the Front Row experience, press Command-Esc (on a Mac laptop, press Fn-Command-Esc) and it takes over your screen (leaving the Mac environment and entering the Front Row environment). You can navigate around, and choose to watch or listen to different things using either your keyboard (use the Up/Down Arrow keys to scroll up and down, and the Return key to enter an area), or you can use that little white wireless remote. So, once you've entered Front Row, use the Arrow keys on your keyboard to scroll down to Photos, then press the Return key (or the Play/Pause button on your remote) to see a list of the photos and slide shows you have in iPhoto. Choose the one you want to see, press the Return key, and it starts playing—full screen, just like you were watching it on TV. When you're done, press the Esc key once to return to the previous screen, or press it three times to exit Front Row.

Emailing Photos (Using Mail)

If you're not using iPhoto and you want to email a photo, it's pretty easy, too. Just click on the photo, and drag it right down to the Mail application icon down in the Dock. This will launch Mail, open a new email message window, and attach your photo to that message, so all you have to do is type in the email address of the person you want to send it to.

X MacTip: How to Keep Emails with Photos from Getting Too Big

Today's digital cameras create photos that are huge in size (for example, a 10-mega-pixel image is approximately 53" wide by 36" deep), and most people don't want you to send them a 53"-wide photo (or if your image is more than 5 MB, your email might be rejected by their email provider). Luckily, you can resize the photo right within Mail, by choosing a new smaller size from the Image Size pop-up menu in the bottom-right corner of the message window (like in the example above, where I lowered the size to Medium).

Make a Photo Your Desktop Background

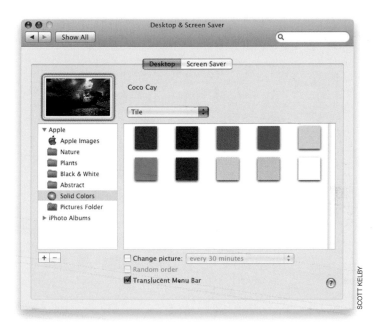

If you see a photo in iPhoto that you'd like to have for your desktop background, just click on it in iPhoto, then go under the Share menu and choose Set Desktop. If the photo you want to use isn't in iPhoto, then do this: Go under the Apple menu and choose System Preferences. When the Preferences dialog opens, click on Desktop & Screen Saver and then click on the Desktop tab. Now simply drag-and-drop the photo you want as your background into the preview window (at the top left), close the dialog, and you're done.

X MacTip: Opening a Photo That Won't Open in iPhoto

If somebody emails you a photo in some format that iPhoto won't recognize, then try dragging-and-dropping it on the Preview icon down in your Dock. Preview will open just about any file format known to modern man, so if it says it doesn't recognize the file type and can't open it, the file is probably damaged, so ask your friend to resend it to you.

Make an iPhoto Album Your Screen Saver

You can use any album of photos you created in iPhoto as your Mac's screen saver, but you don't actually do it from inside iPhoto (well, you make the album there, of course, but you don't make the screen saver there). Instead, you go under the Apple menu and choose System Preferences. When the System Preferences dialog appears, click on Desktop & Screen Saver and then click on the Screen Saver tab. When those preferences appear, in the list of screen savers on the left side, scroll down until you see your iPhoto albums appear in the list. Click on the album you want to use as a screen saver, and on the right it will give you a sample of how your screen saver will look when it's on. You have three different styles you can choose from by clicking on the Display Style buttons at the bottom-left corner of the Preview window. When you find the look you like, just close the dialog (by clicking on the red Close button in the upper-left corner), and now when your screen saver kicks in (after the amount of time you chose with the Start Screen Saver slider near the bottom of the dialog), it will use the photos from the iPhoto album you chose.

More Tips for Using Photos on Your Mac

MacTip: A Great Option for Viewing Your Photos

The next time you have a folder full of photos, don't just look at their icons, try this: first click the Cover Flow button (in the top left of the Finder window—it's the fourth icon under the View section), then click on the little button in the top-right corner of the window. This hides the sidebar and gives the Cover Flow view more room. Now use the horizontal scroll bar at the bottom of the Cover Flow area—or better yet, the Left/Right Arrow keys on your keyboard—to move through your photos. Pretty sweet, eh?

MacTip: Searching for Just the Right Image

If you're searching for a particular photo on your computer, you can narrow your search using the image search that appears near the bottom of any Finder window's sidebar. Under Search For in the sidebar, click on All Images, and then type in your search term in the search field at the top-right corner of the Finder window. A location bar will appear at the top of the main window, where you'll click on All Images again, and now it will only search for images.

MacTip: Having More Than One iChat Photo

When you do a text chat using iChat, if the person you're chatting with is using a Mac, they'll see your photo in the text chat window, and each time you type in a line and hit the Return key, they'll see your photo (so it looks like you talking). The photo it uses is the photo you have in your Address Book (so, if you didn't add a photo of yourself to your Address Book card, you'll have a blue globe icon instead). But, here's the tip—you can have as many iChat photos as you'd like. Just open iChat, and you'll see the current photo it's using as you in the upper-right corner. If you want to add more photos of you (or as a joke, someone else—maybe a celebrity), just drag-and-drop one of them right onto that current photo and it will bring up the iChat photo editor, so you can crop the photo the way you want it. Once you've added some, to choose a different iChat photo, just click once on your photo and a panel will pop down with all your imported iChat photos—just click on the one you want to use and it updates immediately.

MacTip: Sending Large Photos Using iChat

If you want to send someone a photo that's too large to email, then start a chat with them, and send the photo as an attachment by going under iChat's Buddies menu and choosing Send File. Then find the photo you want to send and click the Send button.

Chapter Ten

Getting On the Internet

Anyone Can *Look* at Webpages; Now You Can Make Your Own!

A recent study by the Center for Questionable Studies and Concocted Results just revealed that the number one reason people buy a computer is to get on the Internet. Perhaps even more interesting is that they found the reason people want to get on the Internet is to get on eBay to sell their boat. Apparently, everybody who buys a boat at some point either wants a bigger boat, or they want out, but they certainly don't want the boat they have, and they know darn well none of their friends wants to buy their used boat because they know their friends don't want it. So their only hope is to find someone they don't know—perhaps someone in a different state—to buy their boat, so they go and buy a computer (hopefully a Mac), so they can put the boat up for sale on eBay, and in case you were wondering, this is exactly and precisely how the U.S. economy has stayed so robust for the past 10 or 12 years. Now, I just went to eBay.com, typed in "boat" in the search field, and (I kid you not) it returned 28,273 results, the first being a 2007 Baja Boat Islander Mercruiser and trailer, with only 19 hours of use. This gives you a keen insight into why so many people are buying Macs. This guy had only enjoyed his boat for 19 hours, and he was already on eBay selling it, so he could: (a) get a bigger boat, (b) get rid of his boat, or (c) have an excuse to buy a Mac and get on the Internet. Now, this brings us to you, and my idea for an impromptu study of my own. Here we go: Q. Did you have a boat before you bought your Mac? Q. How many hours after you bought your boat did you begin to want to get on eBay? Q. Did you know that this chapter would show you how to create your own separate webpage to help you sell your boat? Q. Did you know that now you can never sell your Mac, or you'll never really know if your boat sold? These are the things that keep me up at night.

Using the Safari Web Browser

Your Mac has a brilliantly designed Web browser called Safari, which was designed from the ground up to be the fastest browser on the Mac platform, and it has some features that you can only find in it (most folks I know that use Safari can't imagine using anything else). To launch it, just click on its icon in the Dock, and it loads its default homepage. If you want to change the homepage (the page your browser goes to first when you launch it), go under the Safari menu and choose Preferences. Click on the General preferences icon at the top of the dialog, then where it says Home Page, type in any site you'd like and press Command-W to close the Preferences dialog. At the top of Safari is the address bar (where you enter the address of websites you want to visit). The quickest way to enter the address of a different website is to click once on the little icon that appears right before the current website's URL (it's shown circled in red above). This highlights the current URL, so all you have to do is type in a new address, then hit the Return key on your keyboard. If you want to go back to the webpage you were just on, press the Back button (the left arrow), up in the top-left corner of the window.

X MacTip: Save Time Entering Web Addresses

Don't waste time entering the whole "http://www." before a Web address—just type in the name and Safari will put in the rest (i.e., just type Apple.com, or Delta.com, etc.).

Saving a Favorite Page as a Bookmark

If you find a page you want to be able to go back to later, you can save it as a book-mark by going under the Bookmarks menu (up top) and choosing Add Bookmark (you can also just use the keyboard shortcut Command-D). A little dialog will pop down from the top of the page that shows you the title of the site, which is by default how this site will be named. This name isn't always that descriptive, so I always type in something that will make me remember which site this is (for example, there's a site I like to visit that gives safety tips for traveling with photography gear, and it's called *Flying With Fish*. Six months from now, when I go searching through my hundreds of bookmarks, I might not remember that *Flying With Fish* is about photography, so instead, I might name the bookmark "Traveling with Photo Gear"). In that little dialog that pops down, you're also able to choose where to save your bookmark (which we'll talk about on the next page, so for now just leave it set to Bookmarks Menu, as shown here). These bookmarks you save are added to the Bookmarks menu, with your most recently saved bookmark appearing at the bottom of the list (to learn how to change this, turn the page).

Where to Save Bookmarks
(the Menu or Bar?)

When you go to save a bookmark, you have a decision to make: (a) do you want to just add this bookmark to the Bookmarks menu (so the site will be listed in a scrolling list at the bottom of the Bookmarks menu, as shown above), or (b) do you want to add this site to the Bookmarks Bar, where the bookmark for this site appears in the bar up top, to the right of the little Show All Bookmarks icon (it's circled above in red, and looks like an open book), where it's just one click away? Since this bar only has so much room (the width of your browser), I reserve this Bookmarks Bar for sites I visit daily (any other sites I save in the Bookmarks menu instead). So, each time you find a site you like, and choose Add Bookmark (from the Bookmarks menu), you: (1) give the bookmark a name, and then (2) from the pop-up menu below that, you choose whether to add this site to your Bookmarks Bar or your Bookmarks menu. (*Note*: Once you start creating folders, which we'll look at on the next page, you'll then also have the choice of saving your bookmark directly into a bookmarks folder of your choice.)

Organizing Your Bookmarks

When you start bookmarking your favorite sites, it doesn't take long before your Bookmarks menu gets really, really long (or your Bookmarks Bar is packed), so you'll want to create bookmark folders to organize your bookmarks by topic (this helps cut the clutter and gets you to the sites you want faster). For example, I travel a lot, so I have a folder called Travel Stuff with all my travel bookmarks, like United.com, Delta.com, Expedia.com, Starwood.com, etc. To start organizing your bookmarks: (1) First, click on the tiny Show All Bookmarks (open book) icon on the far left of the Bookmarks Bar (it's directly under the Back button), which displays Safari's default bookmarks and folders in the main window. (2) Before you create a new folder, click on Bookmarks Bar (if you want to add a folder to your Bookmarks Bar across the top) or Bookmarks Menu under Collections in the sidebar on the left (as shown here). (3) Now click the little + (plus sign) button in the bottom-left corner of the main window to add a new folder. It appears at the bottom of the list, and its name is already highlighted, so type in whatever name you want for your folder, then press the Return key. (4) To add bookmarks to this folder, just click-and-drag them into the folder (individual site bookmarks are the ones with little icons before their names). That's all there is to it—make a new folder, and drag-and-drop any bookmarked site you want into that folder. To return to the regular webpage view, click on the little open book icon again.

One Click to Load a Folder Full of Sites

One of my favorite features in Safari is called tabbed browsing, because it lets you open up a whole folder full of bookmarked sites with just one click. What's especially cool about this is that while the first site is loading, all the other sites are loading in the background. By the time you're done looking at the first site, the second, third, fourth site, etc., are already fully loaded, so you can check out a bunch of different sites really quickly, with no waiting. Each site appears as its own separate tab, and you just click on the tab to see that site (take a moment and try this once, and I bet you will absolutely love it!). To see how this works, go to a webpage (like Google.com) and do a search for, well…anything. When the results appear, press-and-hold the Command key and click on the first link, and this page will appear in its own separate tab, right up top, to the right of your original site. You can now go back and forth between the two sites by clicking on their tabs. Now, here's where it gets fun: if you Command-click on a bookmark folder up in the Bookmarks Bar, all the sites inside that folder load, each in their own tab. If you always want this, you can set it up to Auto-Click, which does the reverse—if you just click on the folder, it opens all the sites in tabs. If you Command-click, a menu pops up where you can click on an individual site to open. To set up Auto-Click, first click on the Show All Bookmarks icon to bring up the Bookmarks window, then click on Bookmarks Bar at the top of the sidebar on the left to display the bookmarks and bookmark folders you have in the Bookmarks Bar. In the second column of the main window are the Auto-Click checkboxes. Turn on the folder's checkbox, and you're set.

Revisiting Sites You've Already Visited

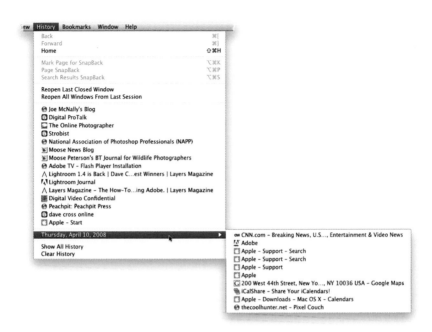

Safari keeps a history of all the sites you've visited, so if you want to go back to a site you went to earlier today, or actually anytime within the past week, just go under the History menu and you'll see a list of today's sites, and then the past seven days' sites are all in folders by day—just hover your cursor over the day you want and all the sites you visited that day will appear in a submenu. To visit one of those sites, just click on it. If you just closed a window (or tab), and want to get back to that same site, go under the History menu and choose Reopen Last Closed Window. If you want to remove a particular site you've visited, go under the History menu and choose Show All History. This takes you to the master listing of all the sites you've visited in the last 30 days. To see a particular day's history, just click on it. To remove a site from your history, click on it, then hit the Delete key on your keyboard. If you want to erase the entire listing of where you've been for the past week, go under the History menu, and at the very bottom of the list, choose Clear History.

Keeping Where You've Been Private

When you browse the Web, four things happen: (1) Safari tracks the History of every site you visit; (2) many sites grab statistics about who's visiting them (that's why when you visit some sites, they start throwing up ads for services in your local area); (3) Safari tracks the name and address of anything you've downloaded from the Web; and (4) anything you searched for using Google is added to the little pop-up search list up in the Google search field in the top-right corner of the Safari window. If you'd rather not have all this personal info tracked (this is especially handy if you're using a shared computer or browsing somewhere public, like the library, or an Internet cafe that rents time on a Mac), then go under the Safari menu and choose Private Browsing before you start visiting sites. This will bring up the warning dialog above, which basically tells you it's not tracking anything. You won't be able to see your History, or see past downloads, or…well, all that stuff. This only lasts until you quit Safari. When you restart it, this feature is turned off.

X | MacTip: Emailing Somebody an Entire Webpage

I'm not talking about emailing a link to a webpage—I'm talking about emailing an entire page, complete with working links. When you're on a site you want somebody else to see, press Command-I and it takes the page you're on, opens Mail, puts the page in an email, puts the name of the site for the subject line, and all you have to do is type in your friend's email address and hit Send. Thanks to my buddy Terry White who turned me on to this very cool tip!

Connecting Your Mac to the Internet

If you're connecting your Mac to the Internet for the first time, start by plugging an Ethernet cable into your Mac's Ethernet port, and then plugging the other end of the Ethernet cable into the input on your high-speed cable or DSL modem. Once the cable is connected, go under the Apple menu and choose System Preferences. When that dialog appears, click on Network (it's in the third row down), and then click on the Assist Me button at the bottom to bring up the Network Setup Assistant (shown above), which will take you through the steps of getting connected to the Internet. In this first screen, you get to name your network (just give it a name that makes sense to you), but before you click the Continue button, make sure you have any information your ISP (Internet Service Provider) gave you to access the Internet using their service, because you may be asked for it in just a minute. Now, when you click the Continue button, it asks you how you're going to connect to the Internet (a wireless AirPort network, cable modem, dial-up telephone connection, etc.), so make your choice and click the Continue button, and depending on what you answered, it may try to connect to the Internet right there on the spot. If you get on—you're set. If it can't connect for some reason, it will ask you for some information to help your Mac get connected.

Use AutoFill to Make Online Shopping Easier

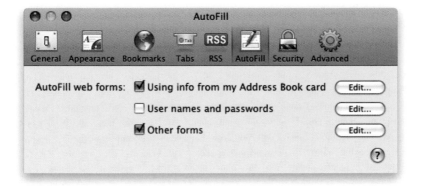

If you're tired of filling out forms from scratch every time you buy something online, then you're going to love Safari's AutoFill feature, which automatically tries to fill in all the stuff you're asked for at lots of online sites (like your name, mailing address, shipping address, phone number, etc.) by accessing the info you entered in your Mac's Address Book. It's a huge time saver, and once you've used it a few times, you'll wonder how you got along without it. When you come to a webpage with a form, press Command-Shift-A and AutoFill will first look on your personal card in Address Book and take the information from there to fill in as much of your online form as it can. If it doesn't find the right info there, it will look in Safari's memory for the last time you filled out a similar online form, and it'll use that instead. If you don't press the AutoFill keyboard shortcut and just start typing, Safari still tries to autofill fields as you type, but if it's not sure what to enter, or if it's not exactly sure of its guess for what you're trying to type, AutoFill will pop-up a little menu with its best guesses. If you see the right info in the list, just click on it, and it enters that info in the form for you. Now, you can make Safari's job easier by making sure you have completely filled out your Address Book card with both your complete home and business addresses (just as you would use if you were filling out an online form). By the way, you can turn this "look in Address Book" feature on/off by going under the Safari menu and choosing Preferences. Click on the AutoFill icon at the top, and then turn on/off the checkbox for Using Info from my Address Book Card.

Finding a Word on a Webpage

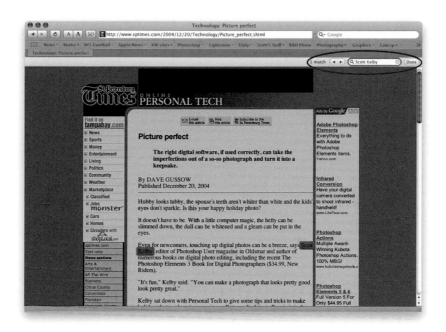

If you come to a webpage and need to find a particular word on that page (for example, let's say you did a Google search for an old friend from your hometown, and you click on one of the results and it brings you to a page from your hometown newspaper, and somewhere on that page is your friend's name), you can have Safari search that page, and not only highlight your word, but if it appears further down the page, it will actually scroll down to that part of the page, and dim everything else so your highlighted word really catches your attention. Just press Command-F and a little search field appears in the top-right corner of Safari's main window (shown circled here in red). Type in a word, and as soon as you start typing, it starts searching (no need to click a button, or hit Return). If it finds your search term on the page, it highlights the first place it finds it in bright yellow (and it lists how many times that term appears on the page). If you press the right arrow button (to the left of the search field; or press Command-G), if your word appears again, it will jump to that instance (each time you press it, it searches further down the page). When you're done searching, either click the Done button (to the right of the search field), or just press the Esc key on your keyboard.

Customizing Safari's Toolbar

Safari comes with a default set of buttons up in the toolbar across the top, but you can set up Safari with just the tools you want (for example, if you find yourself changing onscreen text sizes a lot, you can add Text Size buttons right up there in the toolbar). To do this, go under the View menu and choose Customize Toolbar. The customize dialog pops down from the top of your current window, and in the top row are the individual buttons and tools you can add to Safari's toolbar by simply dragging-and-dropping them up there (here, you can see I've added the Text Size and AutoFill buttons to the toolbar). If you ever want to return to the default set of tools, just click anywhere on the second row down and drag 'em up there. If you want to get rid of something you added (say, you dragged the wrong button up there), just click-and-drag it off the toolbar, and you'll see it disappear in a little puff of smoke. When you're done, click Done.

Connecting to a Wireless Internet Hot Spot

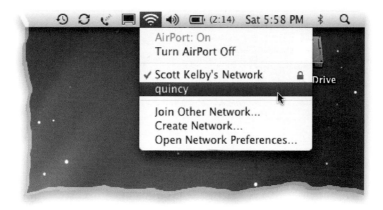

If you want to use your MacBook, MacBook Air, or MacBook Pro to hop on the Internet using an open wireless network found at places like coffee shops, restaurants, hotels, etc., click once on the little radar beams icon on the right side of your Mac's menu bar (it's right near the volume icon), and then from the menu that pops up, choose Turn AirPort On. If there's a wireless network nearby, its name will appear in the section directly below Turn AirPort Off (as seen above, where two wireless networks are within range of my MacBook Pro). If the wireless network you see in this list has a lock icon to the right of it, that's telling you it's a private wireless network, and to use it, you're going to have to have a username and password. If it doesn't have that lock icon, it's an open network (like one you'd find at a hotel, restaurant, etc.), or you have a neighbor with a strong wireless signal, but not real strong feelings about other people hopping on their network for free. Just click on one of these networks to choose it, then launch your Safari Web browser, and you're on the Internet. A word of caution: if you see a third section, below where the wireless networks appear, stay away from those (especially if you see networks called Free Public Wireless or Free WiFi). Those aren't wireless Internet connections—those are thieves trying to fool you into connecting to their nearby laptop, so they can steal personal information off your computer (think identity theft or credit card info theft). So make sure you're not connecting to anything in that third section when you're looking for a free wireless connection.

Creating a Website Using iWeb, Part 1

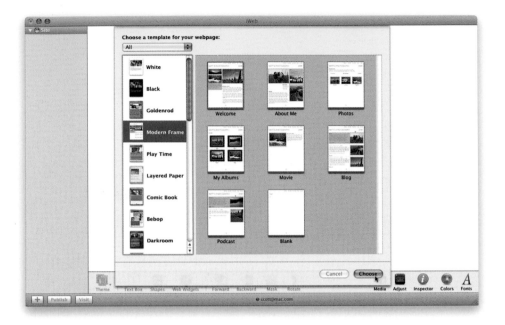

The easiest way to create a professional-looking website is to use Apple's iWeb application (it's in your Applications folder). When you launch iWeb, it brings up the Template Browser, because what you're going to do is choose a theme (a look for your site) and then you're going to replace their photos with your photos, replace their text with your text, and basically use their pre-designed template to create a site the fast and easy way. So, choose a look you like, and then click the Choose button. When you click Choose, your template page opens in iWeb and you'll see all the placeholder text (basically showing you where the text goes) and placeholder photos. Next, you'll learn how to customize your template and make it your own.

X MacTip: Changing Your Theme Later On

If you're building your iWeb website, and you decide the template that you've chosen just isn't working for you (maybe once you put your photos in, the layout didn't match your theme that well), you can easily change themes—just click on the Themes button in the toolbar at the bottom of the iWeb window and choose a different theme.

iWeb: Adding Your Own Text and Photos

The iWeb template

After adding your own text and photos

SCOTT KELBY

When your homepage template appears (shown above left), you'll see the placeholder text and photos. To add your own text, just double-click on any text to select it, and then just type in your own text right over it. This works for headlines, subheads, body copy…you name it. After you're done adding your text, you'll want to add your own photos, too. To add your own photos to your iWeb webpage, click on the Media button down in the toolbar at the bottom of iWeb's window. This brings up a floating Media Browser. Click on the Photos tab at the top, and now you have access to all the photos, events, and albums in your iPhoto library. When you see a photo you want to add to your webpage, just drag-and-drop it onto one of the placeholder photos to replace it with yours. To change the cropping or size of your photo, just click on the photo on the webpage, and a little editor window will appear at the bottom of the photo. You'll see a slider that lets you change the size of the photo inside its box, and if you want to change the position of the photo inside the box (cropping the photo), click the Edit Mask button, then put your cursor right on the photo and click-and-drag it up/down, or left/right to make it fit the way you want it. When you're done, just click anywhere on the page outside of that photo. So, that's all there is to customizing the text and photos on your webpage.

iWeb: Adding Links to Other Sites

If you want to be able to send people reading your website to other pages on the Web (maybe to a news story, or to a friend's website, etc.), just highlight the text you want to be a link, then click the Inspector button at the bottom right of iWeb's window (it's that little blue circle with a white *i* in it). When the Inspector panel appears, click on the Link Inspector icon (the second-to-last icon with the rounded arrow at the top of the panel) to jump to the Link panel (seen above). First, turn on the Enable as a Hyperlink checkbox to make the link live (as shown here). Next, in the Link To pop-up menu, you get to choose whether this link is an external page (like we chose here), where you're linking to somebody else's site; an internal link, where you're linking to one of your own pages; a file, where people can download a file from your webpage; or if the link is an email link, so people can send you email right from your webpage. In our case, we're putting a link to an outside website, so type in the Web address in the URL field. If you want the link to open in a separate window (rather than replacing your page with their page), click the Open Link in New Window checkbox (by the way, anytime I send someone off my site, I always have it open in a new window, so my site stays open in their browser).

X | MacTip: Adding an Email Link So They Can Email You

You add email links pretty much the same way using the same Link panel—just highlight your text (maybe something like "email me"), go to the Links panel again and turn on the Enable as a Hyperlink checkbox, but from the Link To pop-up menu, choose An Email Message. Then type your email address in the To field. Easy enough.

iWeb: Adding More Pages

SCOTT KELBY

If you want to add more pages to your website, just click on the Add button (it's the button with the + [plus sign] down in bottom-left corner of the window). This brings back up the Template Browser, and loads the templates available for the theme you chose. Just click on the type of page you want to add (an About Me page, or a My Albums page, etc.) and when you click Choose, it appears onscreen ready for you to customize (just like you did on the previous page). The cool thing is, since you've added a page to your website, it adds a link at the top of every page, so you can navigate around to different pages (look up in the top-right corner. Before it just had a link to the Welcome page; now there are two links: one to your Welcome [home] page, and one to this About Me page). Each time you add a page, it adds that page link to every page in the site automatically. In the page above, I just started customizing it, so you see mostly placeholder text. Also, if you look at the main photo, you can see I've clicked on it, which brings up that little editor window I mentioned earlier for cropping and resizing your photos.

X MacTip: Adding Movies to Your Webpages

If you have movies you've created in iMovie, or some saved in your Movies folder, you can add them to your webpages just like photos—click on the Media button at the bottom of iWeb's window to get the Media Browser, click on the Movies tab, and drag-and-drop one right onto a placeholder photo.

Creating a Blog Using iWeb

If you want to create a blog (short for weblog), iWeb's got a blog template all ready to go for you. You start like you always would: launch iWeb, and when the Template Browser appears, find a theme you like, but then click on the Blog template. When the blog page appears, you're going to customize the header at the top, just like you would a webpage like we talked about earlier (double-click on the placeholder text to add your own text, and drag-and-drop photos onto your main blog page). The first part of your blog is your main Blog page, which is shown above, and to get to this page, click on the word "Blog" on the top-left side of the iWeb window (it's circled here in red). Now, just double-click on the placeholder text to highlight it and add in your own text, then drag-and-drop your own photos in—basically get the main blog page looking like you'd like. You're only going to edit the top of this page at this point, because the content below the header will be added automatically as you make blog posts (you can see one of my posts in the example shown above. My post is called "Welcome to Lighting Gear Week" and I've got an accompanying photo of me with my post). You create these posts (or entries, as they're called) on the Entries page and they're automatically added to your main Blog page for you (you'll learn how to add entries on the next page).

iWeb: Adding Entries to Your Blog

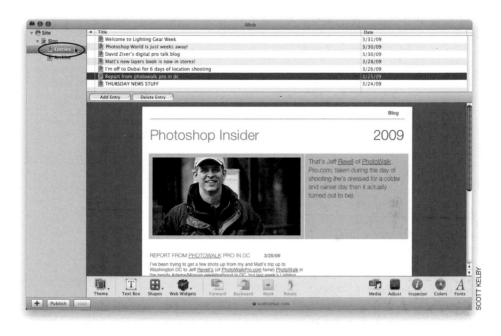

You write your blog posts by clicking on the Entries link (under the main Blog link on the left side of the iWeb window. It's circled here In red). To create a new post (entry), click on the Add Entry button at the top left of the main window, and you get an entry template with a placeholder photo and the headliner text highlighted, ready for you to edit. Double-click the other placeholder text to highlight it and replace it with your own. If you want to add a photo or graphic from iPhoto, click on the Media button at the bottom of the window, find the image in the Media Browser, and drag-and-drop it onto the placeholder photo. It automatically places the date of each post to the right of the post's headline, so if you want to change the date, double-click on it, and a little calendar will pop up so you can choose a different date or format. At the top of the window, you'll see a running list of all your posts, and if you want to edit a particular post, just click on it and it will appear in the main window for you to edit.

iWeb: Creating Your Own Podcast

You build your podcast page just like any other iWeb webpage: Launch iWeb and when the Template Browser appears, find a theme you like, then click on the Podcast page. When the Podcast template appears, double-click on any placeholder text and type in your own text. Now, here's the thing: the page you build here in iWeb is just where your podcast lives on the Web. You still have to create your podcast either in iMovie (if it's a video podcast, which you recorded with a video camera or your Mac's built-in camera) or in GarageBand (for audio-only podcasts). To get these video (or audio) podcasts onto your page, click on the Media button at the bottom of the window to open the Media Browser (shown above). Now, if it's a video podcast, click on the Movies tab, and drag-and-drop the video podcast onto the podcast placeholder on your page (as shown above). If it's an audio podcast, then click on the Audio tab instead, choose your podcast from GarageBand (if that's where you created it) or from iTunes (if you've put it there) and drag-and-drop the podcast onto the placeholder. Once you publish this page (see the next page for how to do that), people who visit your podcast page can watch (or listen) to your podcast right on your webpage.

Putting Your Website, Blog, or Podcast on the Web

You have two choices for how to get your website, blog, or podcast live on the Web: (1) If you have a .Mac account, you can post it there (If you don't have one yet, you can go to www.mac.com and sign up for a free 60-day trial). This is the quickest and easiest way to go, because then you just click the Publish button (in the bottom-left corner of the iWeb window), and it uploads and posts your site (blog, or podcast) live on the Web for you with just that one click (it also gives you the exact Web address of where your site is posted, so you can share it with your friends). Or, (2) you can upload to an existing Web server (maybe you already have a hosting company that hosts your own domain, or maybe you can post it on your company's website, etc.) by going under iWeb's File menu and choosing Publish to a Folder. This puts your website (blog, or podcast) in its own folder, ready for you to upload to your own website. Now, when you update your website (blog, or podcast), if you're using .Mac, you'll need to hit the Publish button again, so the changes you made are updated on your site, blog, or podcast. If you are using your own website, after you make your changes, you'll need to publish to a folder again, and reload your site, blog, or podcast to the Web.

X **MacTip: How to Rename Your Website, Blog, or Podcast**

The name that viewers see within your website's (blog's, or podcast's) Web address, in the address bar of their Web browser, when they visit it is "Site" by default. To change that to a different, more descriptive name, double-click on "Site" in the top-left corner of the iWeb window and type in a different name (don't forget to click on the Publish button to update your website, blog, or podcast).

More Safari Tips

X MacTip: Jumping from Tab to Tab

To jump from open tab to tab (from left to right), press Command-Shift-} (close brace). To go back from right to left, press Command-Shift-{ (open brace). To open a new blank tab, press Command-T.

X MacTip: Marking a Page for SnapBack

If you're doing some research, surfing from page to page, and you come across a page you think you might need later, you don't have to bookmark it (which permanently saves it). Instead just press Command-Option-K (the shortcut for Mark Page for SnapBack). Then, if you need to get quickly back to this page, you don't have to go searching through your History, just press the little Arrow icon at the right end of the address bar and it jumps you back to your last SnapBack page.

X MacTip: Closing a Folder's Worth of Tabs

If you're using tabbed browsing, and accidentally wind up loading a whole folder of sites you didn't mean to, you don't have to wait until they all load, then close them one-by-one. As soon you as realize they're loading, just hit Safari's Back button in the upper-left corner, and it cancels the loading.

X MacTip: Emailing a Web Address

If you want to email someone the Web address for a page you're viewing, just press Command-Shift-I, which launches Mail (or other email program you may be using), and puts the link in a blank email message, all ready go to.

X MacTip: Opening Your Search in a New Tab

When you use Safari's Google search bar, the results replace the window you're currently viewing. However, if you press-and-hold the Command key before you press the Return key to start Google's search, the results will open in a new tab, so your original page stays open in its own tab.

More Safari Tips

X MacTip: Jumping Back Several Sites at a Time

If you click-and-hold on Safari's Back button, a list pops up of the last websites you visited. To jump to one of those, just choose it from the list. The same is true with the Forward button, as well.

X MacTip: Searching Your Bookmarks

When you click the Show All Bookmarks (open book) icon to go to the Bookmarks window, there's a search field that appears in the top-right corner of that window so you can quickly search through your bookmarks. Type in a word, and any bookmarks that contain that word will appear in the window.

X MacTip: Toggling Through Your Bookmarks Bar

If you press Command-1, Command-2, and so on, it will toggle through the individual websites (not folders) you have added to your Bookmarks Bar.

X MacTip: Turning On Safari's Parental Controls

Protect your kids from visiting sites they shouldn't by turning on Safari's parental controls. You do this by going under the Apple menu and choosing System Preferences. In the Preferences dialog, click on Parental Controls, then click on your child's account. When the Parental Controls pane appears, click on the Content tab, and then choose either Try to Limit Access to Adult Web Sites Automatically (the key word here being *try*) or Allow Access to Only These Sites (which I recommend). If you choose that, it brings up a list of default "safe" sites, but you can add your own allowed sites to this list by clicking on the + (plus sign) button at the bottom of the list and typing in the URLs of websites you will allow your child to see.

X MacTip: Searching for Words from Webpages

If you Control-click (or Right-click) on a word you see on a webpage, a pop-up menu appears and you can choose Search in Google to search for that word on the Web, or Look Up in Dictionary for a definition, or Search in Spotlight to search your Mac for files containing that word.

Index

fonts
  email, 105
  iTunes, 142
Force Quit command, 20
Front Row
  playing movies in, 150
  viewing photos in, 205
frozen applications, 20

G

GarageBand, 137–141
  built-in keyboard, 138, 143
  Control menu functions, 139
  creating new projects in, 137
  keyboard shortcuts, 143
  podcast creation in, 230
  pre-recorded loops in, 138–141
  saving songs in, 141
  tuner included in, 143
  working with tracks in, 140, 141
Get Info dialog, 33
Go menu, 4
Google Maps, 82
Google search bar, 232
greeting cards, 189
Grid view, 57
groups
  Address Book, 69–70
  calendar, 83
  iChat, 123
  sending emails to, 82
  Smart Groups, 70

H

hard drives
  ejecting external, 61
  locating files on, 25
  renaming, 28
  retrieving lost files from, 19
  Time Machine backups to, 18
hlding
  sidebar items, 41

  toolbar and sidebar, 60
  Web galleries, 184
  widgets, 90
highlight color, 43
highlighted buttons, 19
History menu, 217

I

iCal, 71–81
  adding events to, 72–73
  blocking out time in, 77
  color-coding calendars in, 76
  Day or Week view, 73, 77
  deleting events from, 73
  editing events in, 72, 73
  Event Editor, 72, 74
  Month view, 72
  moving events in, 74
  publishing calendars in, 81
  reminder alarms in, 75
  repeating events in, 78
  sharing calendars in, 81
  subscriptions in, 80
  switching views in, 75
  tips for using, 83
  To-Do list in, 79–80, 114
  See also **calendars**
iChat, 116–121
  account setup, 116
  audio chat, 121
  Buddy List window, 117
  chat status options, 118, 119
  email indicator, 121
  groups, 123
  photos used in, 209
  sending large photos via, 192, 209
  text chat, 120
  video chat, 121, 151–152
  See also **instant messaging**
icons
  customizing, 33
  moving, 60
  photo thumbnails as, 61